QUICK & HEALTHY LUNCH BOX PLANNER

Great eating they won't want to swap at school

catherine atkinson

D1041800

foulsham

LONDON • NEW YORK • TORONTO • SYDNEY

foulsham

The Publishing House, Bennetts Close, Cippenham, Slough,
Berkshire, SL1 5AP, England

Foulsham books can be found in all good bookshops and direct from www.foulsham.com

ISBN-13: 978-0-572-03262-3
ISBN-10: 0-572-03262-5

Copyright © 2006 W. Foulsham & Co. Ltd

Cover photograph © Terry Pastor

A CIP record for this book is available from the British Library

Printed in Great Britain by Mackays Ltd, Chatham, Kent

CONTENTS

NUTRITIOUS FOOD FOR MIND AND BODY

ew children are enthusiastic about healthy eating, especially when it comes to their school lunchbox. Sending your child to school with food prepared at home should offer a nutritious alternative to school dinners and allow more control over what your child is eating. Despite this, a survey by the Food Standards Agency found that nine out of ten packed lunches contain too much saturated fat, sugar and salt. Peer pressure and outside influences make the demand for crisps, chocolate bars and fizzy drinks inevitable, but there's no in point packing a healthy lunchbox if your child is embarrassed to eat the contents in front of his friends and comes home with them uneaten.

We know that healthy food is vital to children's physical and mental well-being. Children grow rapidly between the ages of five and twelve, gaining an average of 5–7.5 cm (2–3 in) in height each year. To support this growth, they need a good supply of nutrients, especially protein, calcium and iron. Adolescents have higher nutritional needs than any other group, yet often have the poorest diet, preferring the easy option of processed and fast food. Encouraging good food habits from an early age could have a significant effect on health throughout the turbulent teenage years and much later in life. But it's not only a child's body that needs nourishment; key nutrients are vital for the mental skills of concentration, reasoning and learning. High-sugar foods cause fluctuations in blood sugar levels, which can cause mood swings and loss of attentiveness. Slow-release energy foods eaten at lunchtime will help keep your child mentally alert throughout the afternoon.

This book is about striking a balance between a healthy lunchbox and an appealing one. A gradual approach towards healthier eating can be much more effective than a drastic one; foods such as crisps and chocolate don't need to be off-limits, but should be eaten in moderation. It may take a little more planning, but once you get organised it needn't be more time-consuming to pack a healthy lunchbox your child will enjoy.

FINDING THE RIGHT BALANCE

Nutritionists constantly talk about the importance of 'a balanced diet', but it isn't always easy to understand exactly what this means. To grow and to stay healthy, children need to eat a wide variety of foods providing protein, carbohydrates, fats, vitamins, minerals and fibre. Current guidelines state that children and adults alike should eat more starchy foods, more fruit and vegetables, and less fat and sugary foods. Remember, though, that children have slightly different nutritional needs to adults; they need a massive amount of energy-rich food, protein to support their growth and rapid development, and plenty of fruit and vegetables to provide vitamins and protective antioxidants.

Protein

As well as being vital for growth and repair, protein is used to make antibodies and hormones. Because children grow rapidly, they need a higher proportion than adults of protein in their diet. Protein is found in a huge range of foods, including meat and fish, dairy produce and plant sources such as grains, nuts and pulses. Protein from food is broken down during digestion into building blocks known as amino acids. There are twenty-five, but only eight of these are essential (that is, they must be provided by the diet). Animal sources provide all eight, but some amino acids are missing from plant proteins. Don't worry, though, if your child doesn't eat meat or fish; it's possible to combine plant proteins so that amino acids missing in one type will be provided by those in another. For example, cereals lack an amino acid called lysine and most pulses do not contain methionine. If, however, you pack a wheat tortilla filled with a vegetarian bean or lentil pâté, all the amino acids will be present.

Daily protein requirements

Age	Girls	Boys
4–6	20 g	20 g
7–10	28 g	28 g
11–14	41 g	42 g
15–18	45 g	55 g

Protein providers

A matchbox-sized piece of Cheddar	12 g
A pot of fruit yoghurt	5 g
75 g/3 oz roast chicken	20 g
2 lean bacon rashers (slices)	9 g
1 medium egg	7 g
5 almonds	1 g
200 ml/7 fl oz/1 mini carton of milk	7 g

Carbohydrates

From the age of four or five, your child's need for energy-dense foods increases dramatically. Current advice suggests that at least 50 per cent of children's daily energy needs should come from carbohydrates. There are two main groups of carbohydrate: complex (starchy) and simple (refined) sugars. Starchy carbohydrates found in bread, oats, rice, pasta, fruit and vegetables provide slow-release energy and when eaten at lunchtime will keep your child mentally alert throughout the afternoon. (These foods also contain protein and essential minerals and vitamins, particularly those from the B group.)

Most children enjoy sweet, sugary foods and, although sugar provides energy, it raises blood sugar levels quickly, causing peaks and troughs of energy that may lead to mood swings and flagging attention. It isn't realistic to ban all high-sugar foods and allowing small quantities is fine when they are eaten with other foods, but try to limit the number of sugary items in your child's packed lunch. Manufacturers often label their products with technical terms, so when checking the ingredient list, be aware that dextrose, fructose, glucose and sucrose are all types of sugar.

Fat

Children need proportionally more fat in their diets than adults, as it is a concentrated source of energy and the fat-soluble vitamins A and D. However, many foods contain an alarming amount of fat and over-consumption is a major cause of weight and health problems such as diabetes, which can begin at a very early age.

Fats are made up of building blocks of fatty acids and glycerol. There are three types of fatty acids: saturated, polyunsaturated and monounsaturated. Almost all foods that contain fat have a mixture of all three.

Saturated fats are the ones that everyone should cut down on. They are mainly found in food of animal origin – meat and dairy products such as butter and lard (shortening), cream and the fat of meat. Some margarines are made by changing some of the unsaturated fatty acids to saturated ones: these are labelled 'hydrogenated fat' and should be avoided. Try to cut down on 'visible' fats, such as lots of butter on bread and the fat on meat such as bacon and ham, as well as 'hidden' fats in cakes, biscuits and pastries. After the age of five, children can be given some reduced-fat foods such as semi-skimmed milk.

Monounsaturated fats are found in foods such as olive oil, some nuts, oily fish and avocado pears. These may help lower the level of blood cholesterol, so encourage your child to develop a liking for these.

Polyunsaturated fats are the ones we need to include in our diet, which is why they are known as 'essential fatty acids'. There are two types: omega-6, which can be found in sunflower, sesame, walnut and wheatgerm oils and seeds; and omega-3, from soya and rapeseed oil, walnuts and oily fish such as salmon. Both are essential for the functioning of the brain and recent research has shown that the latter may improve concentration and learning.

Fat content of foods

Children need only about 30 g of fat daily; many lunchboxes contain much more than this amount.

Butter or margarine on two slices of bread	16 g
A small bag of crisps	10 g
Two average-sized pork sausages	12 g
Two chocolate digestive biscuits (graham crackers)	4 g
A small bar of chocolate	14 g
A small slice of fruit cake	12 g

Fibre

Fibre is made up of indigestible carbohydrates. It's found in wholefoods such as wholemeal bread, oats, pulses, fruit and vegetables. It passes through the body, absorbing water and waste products and helps move the food through the gut. It is needed to keep your child's digestive system functioning properly. Avoid very high-fibre foods such as bran-based cereals, as they will fill up your child and make it difficult to fulfil her energy needs. Large amounts of fibre can also reduce the absorption of minerals.

Vitamins

Vitamins are vital for growth, development and resistance to illness. With the exception of vitamin D, which is produced by the action of sunlight on the skin, vitamins cannot be made by the body and have to be provided by food. Some can be stored by the body, but others such as the B vitamins and vitamin C need to be supplied on a daily basis.

Nutrition experts are unanimous that children and adults alike should eat more fruit and vegetables – at least five portions a day. These provide vitamin C for immunity and other antioxidant vitamins including A and E that defend the body from the harmful effects of 'free radicals' (which come from pollutants). Fruit and vegetables also contain 'phytochemicals', biologically active compounds that play a vital role in protecting from chronic and life-threatening diseases.

Five-a-day suggestions

Encourage your child to eat five portions of fruit and vegetables daily, whether fresh, canned, frozen or dried. Because it lacks fibre, fruit juice should be counted as only one portion, even if your child drinks more than one glass. Each of the following is 'one portion':

- 2 broccoli spears
- 3 heaped tablespoonfuls of fresh or canned sliced carrots, peas or sweetcorn
- 1 medium-sized (about 75 g/3 oz) serving of salad, such as a handful of carrot, cucumber and celery sticks and a couple of cherry tomatoes
- A small cereal bowl of mixed salad
- 1 medium apple, pear or banana
- 2 satsumas
- 2 medium plums
- 7 strawberries
- A handful of grapes
- A handful of banana chips
- 3 whole dried apricots
- 2 canned peach halves
- 12 canned pineapple chunks
- 3 heaped tablespoonfuls of canned fruit salad
- 1 tablespoonful of raisins or other chopped dried fruit
- A fruity cereal or snack bar
- A medium glass of fruit juice

Minerals

Your child needs a huge range of minerals and these will be provided by a varied diet. Of particular importance are iron and calcium. Iron is vital throughout childhood for both physical and mental development and is often lacking in children's diets. It is even more important for adolescents and it is estimated that at least 17 per cent of teenage girls and 4 per cent of teenage boys suffer from iron deficiency anaemia.

Good sources of iron
- Meat, especially beef, lamb and liver
- Egg yolk
- Canned tuna
- Dried fruit such as apricots
- Fortified breakfast cereals
- Chocolate

Calcium is needed to build strong bones and teeth and your child should have calcium-rich foods every day. As the teenage years approach, this becomes more crucial as this is a time for building up bone density in order to reduce the risk of osteoporosis later in life. Three glasses of milk, a large wedge of cheese or a couple of pots of yoghurt or fromage frais are minimum daily requirements. Semi-skimmed milk has slightly more calcium than whole milk but you do lose out on vitamins A and D.

Good sources of calcium
- Milk, cheese, yoghurt
- Tofu, fortified soya milk
- Broccoli and green leafy vegetables
- White bread and fortified flour
- Canned sardines
- Nuts

Food fads

When your child reaches school age, you will no longer have complete control over what is eaten. Foods that have been previously enjoyed may now be rejected and brought home uneaten. Try not to make an issue out of food fads – nearly all children go through phases of 'picky eating'. It may be due to a genuine dislike of certain foods or perhaps because of peer pressure. Reassure yourself that no single food is essential to health and that, providing your child is growing normally and has plenty of energy, you need not worry too much about short-term food fads. Try to find alternatives to tempt your child; if, for example, cheese and yoghurt are refused, you could try packing a carton of flavoured milk instead.

However, poor eating over a long period of time or a restricted diet (for example, due to cultural reasons or a food intolerance) could eventually result in a vitamin or mineral deficiency and lower resistance to illness. If you are concerned, it may be worth considering a vitamin and mineral supplement. Choose a brand specifically for your child's age group and read the packet carefully.

Dealing with food allergies

Allergies or intolerances to food vary in severity. An allergy is an inappropriate response by the body's immune system to what should be a harmless food. Food intolerance does not affect the immune system and is believed to be caused by an inability to completely digest certain foods. The symptoms of both are similar and may include:

- Nausea and vomiting
- Diarrhoea or stomach pain
- Sneezing, wheeziness and watery eyes
- Blotchy rashes, particularly on the face
- Swelling of the mouth, tongue and face

If your child frequently has these symptoms after eating a certain food, you should consult your doctor. If it is confirmed that there is a problem, it is vital that you let the school know, so it can take immediate medical action if necessary.

The most severe reactions come from nuts (especially peanuts and brazils) and some schools ban these from all packed lunches to protect those children who may react even if they are only in the vicinity of nuts. Other problem foods include seeds, fish and shellfish, egg white, citrus fruits and berries. Should your child be at risk of a severe (anaphylatic) reaction you will be given an emergency injection kit. Make sure that your child has one at school and that there are several members of staff who are trained to administer it.

Coeliac disease results from a sensitivity to gluten, a protein found in cereals, including wheat, rye, barley and oats. It can start at any age and affects around one person in 130. More common in girls than boys, it often runs in families and growth may be affected due to poor absorption of nutrients. There are many gluten-free products including breads, crackers and sweet bakes that can be used in packed lunches.

Lactose intolerance is the inability to digest the sugars in cows' milk. If your child suffers from this it will be necessary to follow a dairy- or lactose-free diet in which soya products are used instead, or goats' milk, which is sometimes tolerated when cows' milk is not. You will need to avoid foods labelled as containing milk, butter, margarine, cheese, cream, yoghurt, casein, caseinates, whey, milk solids, non-fat milk solids and lactose.

PLANNING AND PACKING A LUNCHBOX

Variety and choice are the key to maintaining your child's interest and making sure that the lunch you provide is eaten. However, when preparing a packed lunch becomes a daily event, it can become a struggle to be creative, especially as most people have neither the time nor the inclination in the early-morning rush. A little bit of forward planning and preparation can make this less of a chore and save time in the long run.

- Before you go shopping, consider the packed lunch menu and the meals you will be cooking in the next few days, so that you can plan the balance of food across the whole week. You can save time by linking packed lunches with night-before meals, for example by cooking extra pasta or grilling an additional chicken breast.
- Vary the types of bread you buy and keep a range in the store cupboard; sealed packets of tortilla wraps and pitta breads will usually keep for several weeks. Others such as individual brioches and rolls freeze well and can be split and buttered first, ready for filling.
- Prepare as much as possible the night before; set out the lunchboxes, plastic containers and any utensils needed. Pack anything that won't spoil overnight such as cakes or muffins and unpeeled fruit.
- If lunches are packed the night before, keep perishable foods refrigerated until your child is ready to leave with the lunch.
- If you have a freezer, make the most of it by freezing batches of sandwiches and savoury and sweet bakes, wrapped and ready to pack.

Packing up

When it comes to packed lunches, first impressions count. There are few things worse than unpacking soggy, squashed sandwiches or bruised fruit. For most children, eating lunch isn't a social occasion, it's something to be done quickly so that they can rush out into the playground or take part in lunchtime activities. For this reason, keep lunchbox contents simple to eat and with maximum visual appeal.

There is a huge number of lunchboxes available. While a trendy design and colour may influence your child's choice, other aspects are also important. Make sure that it is big enough to contain all the food and drink that your child needs, but not so large that it's difficult to carry or fit into a school bag. Unless your child's school provides a refrigerated place for keeping lunches cool, consider buying an insulated lunchbox. Alternatively, slip a pre-frozen mini ice pack in with the lunch (remind your child not to throw it away), or freeze a carton or a half-filled plastic bottle of drink (top it up with extra cold water in the morning). The ice will keep the food cool, but will have melted in time for lunch. Wash the lunch container with hot water and detergent after every use, unless the label states otherwise in which case you should spray it with an anti-bacterial cleaner and wipe it clean with kitchen paper (paper towels).

Use clingfilm (plastic wrap) or greaseproof (waxed) paper and foil, or plastic bags to wrap foods, or pack in separate small plastic boxes. Make sure that packets and containers are easy to open, as it can be frustrating for a child to have to wait for assistance from the midday supervisor. Remember to include a piece of kitchen paper (paper towel) or a wrapped moist wipe for sticky fingers, plus a fork or spoon to accompany foods such as salads or desserts.

Drinks

The array of cartons and bottles of flavoured drinks and fruit squashes, colourfully packaged with pictures of cartoon characters are tempting, but even those enriched with vitamins and minerals to make them more marketable should really only be included in the lunchbox as an occasional treat. Water, whether plain tap, filtered or mineral is still the best choice for your child. It plays a vital part in efficiently relaying signals between brain cells, and insufficient water causes mild dehydration, making learning more difficult. In recognition of this, many schools now allow children to keep bottled water on their desks during lesson time.

Fruit juices may seem like a healthy choice, but most have added sugar and preservatives. Even those that are 100 per cent juice still contain natural sugar and have a high acidity content, which will contribute to tooth decay. Fruit juices lack many of the benefits of whole fruit, including fibre content, so it is preferable to send a combination of fresh fruit and water. Some children however, would rather go thirsty than settle for water! If this is the case, pack 'pure' fruit juice, 'toothkind' squash or a carton of milk.

Involving your children

It can be frustrating when some of the lunch you've carefully prepared is brought home uneaten or swapped in the playground. Most children are influenced by their peers and advertising and don't want to appear different, so it makes sense to ask them what their friends eat and what they'd like included in their lunchbox. Chatting about the contents will help them learn about nutrition and enable you to strike a balance between a healthy lunchbox and one that is acceptable and fun. Many schools have a policy of not allowing children to dispose of any uneaten foods, so you can see what has been left. If your child regularly brings home the healthier foods you may need to reduce overall quantities and 'treat' items.

A balanced meal in a box

Over a third of a child's nutrient needs should be met by lunch. To help you plan a weekly menu, it's useful to follow the national guidelines set for primary schools. These suggest that the midday meal should contain:

- One portion of vegetables or salad and one portion of fruit (this may be fresh, dried or canned).
- One portion of a milk or dairy item such as milk, cheese, yoghurt, fromage frais or a yoghurt drink.
- One portion of meat, chicken, fish, eggs, peanut butter, beans or another protein source.
- One portion of starchy food such as bread, pasta, rice, noodles or potatoes.

Weekly meal planner

Monday

- 1 Soft White Milk Bap (see page 134) filled with Egg Mayonnaise (see page 33) and sliced cucumber
- 1 slice of Chewy Oat and Syrup Flapjack (see page 114)
- 1 small apple or pear
- A mini tub or tube of fromage frais
- A bottle of plain water or carton of pure orange juice
- Extra for large appetites: Savoury Wheat and Oat Shortbread (see page 133)

Tuesday

- Mini Meatballs with Minted Yoghurt Dip (see page 77) or Dutch Cheese and Carrot Salad **V** (see page 62)
- A buttered mini pitta bread
- A handful of cherry tomatoes
- Fresh and Fruity Orange Jelly (see page 102) or Mixed Fresh Fruit Kebabs (see page 101)
- A bottle of plain or flavoured water
- Extra for large appetites: 1 Smart Oat and Raisin Cookie (see page 120) or a few fat-reduced crisps or potato snacks

Wednesday

- Smoked Salmon and Taramasalata Wrap (see page 39) or Tabbouleh with Feta Cheese **V** (see page 58)
- A few sticks of carrot and cucumber
- 1 Raspberry Yoghurt Muffin (see page 110)
- A bottle of plain water or squash
- Extra for large appetites: 1 Fruit and Nut Energy Bar (see page 112) or a bought cereal/dried fruit bar

Thursday

- Shredded Chicken with Lemon Coleslaw (see page 56)
- or Creamy Vegetable Soup **V** (see page 96)
- 1 buttered Cheese and Oatmeal Roll (page 136)
- 1 Mini Chocolate-chip Muffin (see page 111)
- A few grapes or a small banana
- A carton of plain or flavoured milk
- Extra for large appetites: 1 Sausage and Tomato Sauce Spiral (see page 132) or a couple of rice cakes

Friday
- 1 Crispy Bacon Brioche Finger (see page 51) or 2 slices of brioche loaf or 1 brioche roll with Lentil and Soft Cheese Pâté *V* (page 92)
- A few celery sticks
- 1 slice of Fresh Apple and Apricot Traybake (see page 116)
- A yoghurt drink or smoothie and a bottle of water
- Extra for large appetites: 1 mini cheese and a couple of sesame breadsticks

Easy extras

Include a few items from this list to add variety to lunchtime and satisfy hunger pangs. Some are simple to assemble at home; others may be bought from the supermarket ready-prepared and wrapped.

- Mini cheeses
- Cheese strings
- Cold cooked mini sausages
- Mini tubs or tubes of fromage frais
- Individual yoghurts or probiotic yoghurt drinks
- Small pots of rice pudding
- A couple of plain or sesame breadsticks, rice cakes or oatcakes
- A small sealed container of popcorn (microwave popcorn can be made fresh on the day)
- Mini boxes of raisins
- Individual bags of dried apricots
- Pumpkin and sunflower seeds
- Small bunches of seedless grapes
- A handful of strawberries
- Apple wedges, tossed in orange juice
- Cubes of melon, papaya (pawpaw) and mango
- Carrot, celery or cucumber sticks and a few cherry tomatoes
- A few crisps, potato snacks or mini poppadoms (preferably low-fat) in a small container
- Baby bananas
- Satsumas, tangerines or clementines (peel and wrap in clingfilm (plastic wrap) for younger children)
- A cereal or dried fruit bar

BEGIN WITH BREAKFAST

After a night's sleep, blood sugar levels are at their lowest, so get your child's day going with a good breakfast to keep concentration levels up and to stave off hunger pangs until lunchtime. Try to make sure that you allow enough time for your child to eat in the morning. Breakfast doesn't have to be substantial to be nutritious. This is a good time to have at least one portion of the daily recommended five servings of fruit and vegetables. A balanced breakfast should contain the following:

- About 25 per cent of your child's daily calorie intake
- A reasonable amount of protein
- Plenty of starchy carbohydrates
- Some calcium, iron and vitamin C
- Only a small amount of fat and sugar

This is not as difficult as it might seem and can be achieved by serving a small glass of fruit juice, a bowl of unsweetened cereal with whole or semi-skimmed milk and a slice of wholemeal toast with peanut butter.

Better breakfasts

Many children will eat a bowlful of the same breakfast cereal every morning. Encourage them to try something different occasionally to achieve a balanced diet. Sugar-coated cereals aren't ideal as they encourage children to develop a sweet tooth, so try to make them an occasional treat, perhaps at the weekend.

- Traditional porridge or instant oats that are mixed with hot milk are great breakfast fodder, providing slow-release energy and vital vitamins and minerals. A scattering of chopped fresh fruit or soaked dried fruit or a small glass of fruit juice will make this a nutrient-rich choice.
- A 'cooked' breakfast of an egg or some grilled bacon is fine occasionally and will provide a good amount of protein and iron, but

it's important to eat some complex carbohydrates for sustained energy as well, so add some toast or lightly buttered bread and some vitamin-C rich fruit juice to help absorb the iron. (Some children find orange juice very acidic first thing in the morning, so try pear, apple or tropical fruit juice for a change.)

- For a light, calcium-rich breakfast, serve some fruit-flavoured or Greek-style yoghurt drizzled with honey and a sprinkling of crunchy cereal.
- Some days your child's appetite may be poor, perhaps because of excitement about a school trip or exam nerves. Encourage him to have something, even if it is just a glass of warm milk. Alternatively, pack a cereal snack bar to eat at break time.

Super smoothies

Smoothies are satisfying yoghurt or milk and fruit drinks, especially good on hot summer days. They are ideal for children who can't face a big breakfast before school and make an almost perfect 'meal in a glass' with a good amount of protein, calcium and B and C vitamins.

Banana smoothie

Blend 1 small sliced banana with a 150 g/5 oz carton of orange or tropical fruit yoghurt and 120 ml/4 fl oz/½ cup of semi-skimmed milk. For a banoffee smoothie, blend the banana with a 150 g/5 oz carton of toffee yoghurt and 120 ml/4 fl oz/½ cup of semi-skimmed milk. Dust a little drinking (sweetened) chocolate powder over the top.

Mango smoothie

Peel half a mango and cut the flesh away from the stone (pit). Chop the flesh roughly and put it in a food processor or blender. Process until fairly smooth. Add a 150 g/5 oz carton of natural yoghurt, 120 ml/ 4 fl oz/½ cup of semi-skimmed milk and 5 ml/1 tsp of clear honey. Blend until smooth and frothy.

Raspberry and kiwi smoothie

Blend 100 g/4 oz of fresh raspberries and 1 peeled and chopped ripe kiwi fruit with a 150 g/5 oz carton of raspberry yoghurt and 120 ml/ 4 fl oz/½ cup of semi-skimmed milk.

AFTER-SCHOOL SNACKS

When children come home from school ravenous, try to avoid reaching for the biscuit tin and offer some of these satisfying snacks instead.

- Bread, a great source of starchy carbohydrate, also contains B vitamins, iron and calcium. Serve fresh or toasted slices of wholemeal or 'whole white' with peanut butter or soft cheese, topped with a little good-quality jam (conserve). Breadsticks, rice cakes and oatcakes are good alternatives.
- A pot of 'trail mix' – dried fruits such as apricots, mango, sultanas (golden raisins) and raisins, and pumpkin and sunflower seeds (keep a jar ready-made in the cupboard). These are great energy boosters and are packed with concentrated vitamins and iron.
- Fresh fruit such as grapes, apples and pears, great for vitamins and antioxidants, or a banana, a concentrated source of energy and the mineral potassium, vital for muscle and nerve functions.
- A 'healthy' home-made muffin, cake or other bake (unlike the shop-bought equivalent, it will be additive-free).
- A fruit smoothie or, on cold days, a cup of hot chocolate made with semi-skimmed milk.

GOING ON A PICNIC

Another big advantage of all these recipes is that they make perfect picnic food. Whether your picnic has been planned well in advance or is a spur-of-the-moment decision, the pleasures of outdoor eating are unbeatable, whatever the weather. Make sure that nothing spoils your day out by getting organised before you set off, so that you arrive at your destination with all your food and drink in good condition and with nothing missing.

Planning the menu

The secret of a successful picnic is simplicity. It's important to choose foods that will travel well and which will remain in peak condition, especially in hot weather. Sandwiches may be the ultimate portable meal, but there are plenty of other options. Finger food is ideal and avoids the need for lots of different cutlery and plates, which are heavy to carry and will need washing up afterwards. Themed picnics are fun for children, particularly if they are inviting friends; a 'teddy bear's picnic' is an obvious choice, but you could try a jungle-style or pirate picnic.

- Take a selection of double-decker sandwiches (see page 36) and/or some savouries such as Mini Meatballs with Minted Yoghurt Dip (see page 77) and Sweet and Sticky Chicken Skewers (see page 74) or Picnic Pies with Herb and Tomato Sausage Filling (see page 84).
- Add some salad, such as Tabbouleh with Feta Cheese (see page 58) or Dutch Cheese and Carrot Salad (see page 62) packed in individual plastic lidded bowls that can double up as serving dishes. Alternatively, take some vegetable crudités such as carrots and cucumber or buy a bag of prepared washed salad from the supermarket and take a screw-topped jar of dressing to add just before serving.
- Take one or two snack items such as Sausage and Tomato Sauce Spirals (see page 132) or Savoury Wheat and Oat Shortbread (see page 133) cut into fun shapes for a themed picnic. Or, if preparation

time is short, pack some lower-fat crisps or a healthy snack such as unroasted peanuts and raisins.

● Pots of yoghurt, fromage frais or mousse make an easy dessert. Alternatively, take some Mixed Fresh Fruit Kebabs (see page 101) or Fresh and Fruity Orange Jelly (see page 102).

● For big appetites, bakes such as Moist Carrot Cup Cakes (see page 106) or Chewy Oat and Syrup Flapjacks (see page 114) will ensure no one goes hungry.

● Mini cartons of drinks are easy for small hands to hold, but large cartons or bottles of water or fruit juice are more economical (remember to take plastic cups and straws too). Avoid fizzy drinks such as sparkling water, unless there is plenty of time for them to settle after the journey before being opened.

Food for the active

Keen cyclists and walkers will need lots of energy-giving food to keep them going. With space at a premium and a need to keep the picnic as light as possible, you won't want to carry plates or heavy empty containers. Choose robust rolls such as Big Brunch Sausage Bap (see page 48) or Spiced Turkey and Vegetable Calzone (see page 86) rather than flimsy sandwiches, which can be simply packed in plastic bags. (Pack from frozen or with a half-frozen drink, so that you won't need an ice pack.) Choose high-energy savouries such as Crispy-coated Sausage Nuggets (see page 76) and sweet bakes such as Fruit and Nut Energy Bars (see page 112).

Packing the picnic

Rigid plastic boxes or tins will keep the food fresh and protect more delicate items from being squashed. Greaseproof (waxed) paper overwrapped with clingfilm (plastic wrap) or foil will keep individual items in peak condition. The food should all pack neatly into a large coolbox or insulated bag. Remember to pack in reverse order, starting with the dessert and placing the sandwiches and savouries on top. Make sure that drinks are easily accessible, as this is likely to be the first thing your child asks for when you stop to eat.

Picnic checklist

Write a list of items you'll need for your picnic and tick them as you pack.

- Food: keep this in the fridge until the last moment. It's a good idea to clear a shelf in the fridge just for the picnic items, so you can make sure you've got everything. Some items such as small cakes are best packed from frozen, so make sure you leave a prominent note to remind you to pack them.
- Cold drinks and/or a flask of tea or coffee and milk or coffee whitener and sugar.
- Cutlery: forks for eating salad; teaspoons for yoghurts and jellies and for stirring hot drinks; a sharp knife for cutting (with the blade carefully wrapped in kitchen paper secured with an elastic band).
- Plates, bowls, mugs and glasses: these may be paper for easy disposal, although plastic ones are a worthwhile investment if you regularly go on picnics.
- Kitchen paper (paper towels), wet wipes or a damp cloth for hands and faces.
- Clingfilm (plastic wrap) or plastic bags for leftovers.
- A picnic rug or groundsheet; a wind break (especially for sandy beaches); an umbrella for shade.
- A plastic bag for rubbish.
- A first aid kit.

Safe eating

- Always wash your hands before preparing food and eating it. Take antiseptic disposable wipes with you if washing facilities are unlikely to be available.
- Pack chilled food in a coolbox or an insulated bag. If the weather is hot, either use several ice packs or freeze almost-filled plastic bottles with squash or water (these can also be used for drinks).
- Make sure foods such as chicken and sausages are thoroughly cooked. Cool them quickly after cooking and chill in the fridge as soon as they are cold.

Remember to ...

- Check the opening and closing times of venues such as zoos, parks and gardens.
- Make sure you have enough petrol, oil and water in the car before you depart, or that you have a timetable for public transport, and a map and mobile phone if necessary.
- Pack a ball, frisbee or games to play and a camera.

NOTES ON THE RECIPES

- Do not mix metric, imperial and American measures. Follow one set only.
- American terms are given in brackets.
- The ingredients are listed in the order in which they are used in the recipe.
- All spoon measurements are level: 1 tsp = 5 ml; 1 tbsp = 15 ml.
- Eggs are medium (size 3) unless otherwise stated. If you use a different size, adjust the amount of liquid added to obtain the right consistency.
- Always wash, peel, core and seed, if necessary, fresh foods before use. Ensure that all produce is as fresh as possible and in good condition. Use organic produce where possible.
- Salt and pepper are included in many recipes, but you should avoid over-seasoning with salt and preferably use a low-sodium version. Only add pepper if your child likes it. The use of strongly flavoured ingredients such as garlic and ginger also depends on personal taste and quantities can be adjusted accordingly.
- Always use fresh herbs unless dried are specifically called for. If it is necessary to use dried herbs, use half the quantity stated. Chopped frozen varieties are much better than dried. There is no substitute for fresh parsley or coriander (cilantro).
- Use any good-quality oil, such as sunflower, corn or groundnut (peanut), unless olive oil is specifically called for.
- Use butter or margarine of your choice in the recipes. Since some margarines or spreads are best for particular uses, check the packet before use.
- Can and packet sizes are approximate and will depend on the particular brand.
- Use whichever kitchen gadgets you like to speed up preparation and cooking times: mixers for whisking; food processors for grating, slicing, mixing or kneading; blenders for liquidising.

- All ovens vary, so cooking times have to be approximate. Adjust cooking times and temperatures according to manufacturer's instructions.
- Always preheat a conventional oven and cook on the centre shelf unless otherwise specified.
- Vegetarian recipes are marked with a V symbol. Those who eat fish but not meat will find plenty of additional recipes containing seafood. Some vegetarian recipes contain dairy products; omit them or substitute with a vegetarian alternative if you prefer. Recipes may also use processed foods and vegetarians should check the specific product labels to be certain of their suitability, especially items such as pastry (paste), breads, stock cubes, jellies (jello) and chocolate products.
- Recipes containing nuts are marked with an N symbol. Read the relevant notes on nut allergies on page 15.
- Use your own discretion in substituting ingredients and personalising the recipes. Make notes of particular successes as you go along.

SENSATIONAL
SANDWICHES

Sandwiches are still the mainstay of packed lunches and it's amazing what you can pack between two slices of bread. This chapter has dozens of ideas for different fillings, not only traditional ones but plenty of more unusual ideas that are destined to become your child's new favourites. Remember that sandwiches don't have to be limited to two slices of bread and a single filling; here you'll find suggestions for alternative ways to present them, such as layered 'double-decker' sandwiches.

Next time you're in the supermarket or bakery, have a look at the vast number of different types of breads and rolls available. Try multi-grain, crusty rolls, soft finger rolls, brioche, ciabatta, baps, pittas, naans, bagels, focaccia, mini baguettes, soda farls, tortilla wraps and croissants. You'll also find new types of 'child-friendly' sliced loaves available, including a clever crustless variety and a 'whole white' bread with added wheatgerm, which has the nutritional advantages of wholemeal bread but without the heavy texture. Bread made with barley or rye flour or oatmeal is delicious for a change. Even less adventurous children can get bored with the same daily packed lunch; but the ubiquitous sliced cheese filling can taste very different if served in simple sliced white bread one day, a seeded crusty bap with pickle the following day and in a pocket of pitta bread with shredded salad the next.

Professional tips for sandwich making

I don't doubt you know how to make a sandwich but you'll find these professional tips really useful as they'll help you to make really super sandwiches. Remember that you need them to keep and travel and still be at their best at lunchtime. Plus you need to optimise use of your valuable time in the morning.

- Ease the early-morning rush by making sandwich fillings such as egg or tuna and sweetcorn mayonnaise the night before. Some such as plain cheese or ham may be completely prepared, but avoid adding moist or salad ingredients.
- Have a supply of rolls or sliced bread in the freezer for those occasions when you haven't had time to shop or have forgotten to add bread to your list. Frozen bread can be used to make sandwiches in the morning and will have defrosted by lunchtime. Keep store cupboard standbys as well, such as cans of tuna or ham.
- If buttering the bread, soften the butter first so it is easier to spread sparingly.
- Avoid soggy sandwiches by drying salad ingredients such as lettuce. After washing, pat on kitchen paper (paper towels) to soak up excess moisture.
- Sandwiches don't have to be square; try triangles or fingers. On special days or when your child first starts school, cutting sandwiches into fancy shapes with a biscuit (cookie) cutter will make them fun to eat.

- Keep sandwiches fresh and retain flavour by wrapping them in clingfilm (plastic wrap) or greaseproof (waxed) paper, then silver foil as soon as you have made them. Alternatively, buy sandwich bags or plastic boxes with snap-on lids. Keep refrigerated until the last minute.
- Many sandwiches can be made in advance and frozen. Fillings that freeze well include sliced meat, chicken and fish, hard cheeses, cheese spreads and peanut butter. Don't freeze sandwiches with fillings made with hard-boiled (hard-cooked) eggs, mayonnaise, salad cream, soft low-fat cheeses such as ricotta, salad or fresh fruit.

Favourite fillings

There will be times when you want to go back to old favourites, and here are some of mine – and I hope they include yours too! Making sandwiches does not have to be difficult. Start with the basics and make your own adjustments depending on the fresh foods you have available at the time. See also Classic Club Sandwich with Chicken, Bacon and Tomato on page 37.

- **Apple, cheese and celery:** coarsely grate ½ a crisp apple and mix immediately with 10 ml/2 tsp of salad cream to stop it browning. Stir in ½ a grated carrot and 25 g/1 oz/¼ cup of grated Double Gloucester or Red Leicester cheese.
- **BLT:** roughly crumble 2 crisply grilled (broiled) back or streaky bacon rashers (slices) and mix with 30 ml/2 tbsp of shredded lettuce and 1 sliced tomato.
- **Creamy salmon and watercress:** mix half a 210 g/7½ oz/small can of pink salmon or 100 g/4 oz flaked cooked fresh salmon with 30 ml/ 2 tbsp of crème fraîche and a small handful of chopped watercress.
- **Crispy bacon and peanut butter:** spread crunchy peanut butter (see page 98 or use bought) on one slice of bread. Scatter with 2 chopped crisply grilled (broiled) back or streaky bacon rashers (slices) and top with the second slice of bread. *N*
- **Crunchy alfalfa and chicken:** lay one slice of roast chicken (or turkey) on the bread, spread thinly with mayonnaise or salad cream, then scatter with a handful of alfalfa (see page 72 for sprouting your own beans).
- **Egg mayonnaise:** finely chop 1 hard-boiled (hard-cooked) egg with 10 ml/2 tsp of mayonnaise and a little salt and pepper. Add some salad cress for colour and texture.

- **Egg and tomato:** slice 1 hard-boiled (hard-cooked) egg and 1 tomato. Arrange them in layers on lettuce-lined bread and spread thinly with mayonnaise or salad cream.
- **Hummus, cucumber and carrot:** mix 30 ml/2 tbsp of hummus (see page 68 or use bought) with 4 slices of finely chopped cucumber and ½ a carrot, coarsely grated (squeeze out excess juice from the carrot before mixing).
- **Mustard beef:** spread 1 slice of roast beef with 10 ml/2 tsp of mayonnaise mixed with 1.5 ml/¼ tsp of mild mustard or creamed horseradish.
- **Peanut butter, apple and raisins:** thickly spread the bread (oatmeal bread is particularly good) with peanut butter (see page 98 or use bought), top with ½ a sliced apple, tossed in orange juice, then scatter with 10 ml/2 tsp of raisins. *N*
- **Prawn cocktail:** blend 15 ml/1 tbsp of mayonnaise with 5 ml/1 tsp of tomato ketchup (catsup) or purée and a squeeze of lemon juice. Mix in 50 g/2 oz of cooked, peeled prawns (shrimp) (pat them dry first on kitchen paper) and 30 ml/2 tbsp of finely shredded little gem lettuce.
- **Ricotta cheese with dates and walnuts:** blend 25 g/1 oz/2 tbsp of ricotta cheese with 5 ml/1 tsp of runny honey and use instead of butter on the bread. Scatter with 50 g/2 oz/⅓ cup of chopped fresh dates and 25 g/1 oz/¼ cup of finely chopped walnuts. *N*
- **Sausage and chutney:** slice a cold cooked sausage lengthways and spread with 15 ml/1 tbsp of tomato chutney.
- **Soft cream cheese and smoked salmon:** spread one slice of lightly buttered brown bread with 25 g/1 oz/2 tbsp of softened cream cheese blended with a few snipped chives, if liked. Top with one or two slices of smoked salmon (look out for smoked salmon trimmings, which are good value) and 4 slices of cucumber.
- **Swiss cheese and honey-roast ham:** place one slice of honey-roast ham on a slice of lightly buttered bread and spread with mayonnaise or salad cream. Lay 4 slices of cucumber on top, then a thin slice of Swiss cheese. Top with the second slice of bread.
- **Tuna and sweetcorn:** mix 90 g/3½ oz/½ small can of drained tuna with 15 ml/1 tbsp of drained canned or thawed frozen sweetcorn and 15 ml/1 tbsp of mayonnaise and a squeeze of lemon juice. If liked, add extras such as finely chopped red (bell) pepper (or buy canned sweetcorn with added pepper), cucumber and spring onions (scallions).

- **Tuna, tomato and avocado:** mix 90 g/3½ oz/½ small can of drained tuna with 10 ml/2 tsp of mayonnaise and 1 finely chopped tomato. Toss ¼ chopped ripe avocado in 5 ml/1 tsp of lemon juice and mix together.

Sandwich spreads

Spreading butter or margarine on your bread stops moist fillings soaking into it and makes the sandwich more palatable. But you don't have to stick with butter; for a change, try jazzing it up with simple flavourings and freezing in small portions.

If the filling comprises avocado, hummus, cottage cheese or a generous amount of mayonnaise, it isn't necessary to spread the bread with butter or margarine. Make sure, though, that a dryish ingredient such as lettuce or sliced cheese is next to the bread to stop it soaking up too much moisture.

- **Cheese and tomato butter:** beat 25 g/1 oz/¼ cup of finely grated Cheddar cheese and 5 ml/1 tsp of tomato purée (paste) into 50 g/ 2 oz/¼ cup of softened butter or margarine.
- **Mild mustard butter:** beat 2.5–5 ml/½–1 tsp of wholegrain or mild French mustard into 50 g/2 oz/¼ cup of softened butter or margarine.
- **Savoury butter:** beat 5 ml/1 tsp of vegetable or beef extract such as Marmite or Bovril into 50 g/2 oz/¼ cup of softened unsalted (sweet) butter.

Double-decker sandwiches

Made with three slices of bread, these are a great way to encourage your child to eat brown or wholemeal (wholewheat) bread. They're also a fun way to combine different flavoured fillings and are great for parties. Choose ingredients with contrasting colours that work well together. For easy eating, use thinly sliced bread and finely chopped fillings. See Chicken, Cream Cheese and Cucumber Double-decker on page 38 for how to assemble a double-decker sandwich.

- Crunchy peanut butter and seedless raspberry or smooth strawberry jam (conserve). *N*
- Flaked canned crabmeat mayonnaise with ricotta cheese and thinly sliced tomato.
- Flaked cold cooked or smoked salmon and cream cheese with snipped chives.
- Lean roast beef or pastrami and shredded salad with mild mustard mayonnaise.
- Mashed sardines and ketchup (catsup) and cream cheese mixed with a finely chopped cornichon.
- Sliced mild cheese and smoked or honey-roast ham.
- Smoked chicken or turkey with cranberry sauce and wafer-thin slices of Brie.

This substantial sandwich is ideal for an older child or one with
a large appetite, or you could use just one rasher of bacon and
thinly sliced bread. Sandwiches are made several hours in
advance, so they need to keep and travel well; placing moister
fillings between drier ones stops the bread becoming soggy.

classic club sandwich
with chicken, bacon and tomato

MAKES 1

Softened butter or margarine	2 crisply grilled (broiled) bacon
2 medium-thick slices of bread	rashers (slices)
A few little gem lettuce leaves	1 tomato, sliced
1 slice of chicken breast	10 ml/2 tsp mayonnaise

1   Thinly butter one side of each slice of bread and place, butter-side
up, on a chopping board.

2   Lay half the lettuce leaves on one slice and top with the chicken
and bacon. Arrange the tomato slices on top and spread with the
mayonnaise.

3   Top with the remaining lettuce leaves, then the second slice of
bread.

Most children like cream cheese, and with the chicken this makes an excellent, protein-filled sandwich to keep your child alert and full of energy through the afternoon. The flavours are quite mild, so adding a little seasoning is a good idea as long as your child likes it. The cucumber adds a nice crunch.

chicken, cream cheese and cucumber double-decker

MAKES 1

Softened butter or margarine
2 thin slices of white bread
1 thin slice of wholemeal bread
25 g/1 oz/2 tbsp soft cream cheese
1 cm/½ in slice of cucumber,
   finely diced

40 g/1½ oz cooked chicken,
   finely shredded
10 ml/2 tsp mayonnaise
2.5 ml/½ tsp tomato purée (paste)
Salt and pepper (optional)

1 Very thinly butter one side of each slice of white bread and butter the wholemeal bread on both sides. Mix together the cream cheese and cucumber and spread over one of the white bread slices, then top with the wholemeal slice.

2 Mix the chicken with the mayonnaise and tomato purée and a little salt and pepper, if liked. Spread over the wholemeal bread slice, then top with the remaining slice of white bread.

3 Using a sharp knife, remove the crusts and cut the sandwich into three strips or four squares. Wrap straight away with clingfilm (plastic wrap) or foil and keep chilled until ready to pack.

Wraps are a child-friendly way of containing moister and chunkier fillings. You'll find them in the 'exotic food' aisle or bread section in most supermarkets. Soft flour and corn tortillas (the 30 per cent corn flour makes them golden) are ideal, or try crêpes or pancakes. Warm the wraps to make them pliable.

smoked salmon
and taramasalata wrap

MAKES 1

1 large tortilla, about 20 cm/8 in	8 very thin slices of cucumber
30 ml/2 tbsp taramasalata	Finely shredded lettuce (optional)
50 g/2 oz smoked salmon	

1 Lay out the tortilla on a board and spread with the taramasalata. Arrange the smoked salmon on top.

2 Cut the cucumber slices in half to make them easier to roll up, and place these on top of the salmon. Scatter with shredded lettuce, if using.

3 Roll up the tortilla like a parcel, tucking in the ends before you start rolling (this will help to stop the filling falling out when the wrap is eaten). Wrap tightly in clingfilm (plastic wrap) and keep chilled until ready to pack.

This is a good choice for busy households as making the filling in advance reduces the inevitable early-morning rush to leave the house on time. You could make two or more of these and enjoy one for your own lunch! Using clingfilm rather than foil keeps the wrap soft and easy to eat.

chicken fajita wrap
with greek-style yoghurt

MAKES 1

15 ml/1 tbsp sunflower or light
  olive oil
A pinch of ground paprika
5 ml/1 tsp lemon juice
30 ml/2 tbsp Greek-style yoghurt
Salt and pepper
100 g/4 oz chicken breast,
  cut into strips

$\frac{1}{2}$ small onion, thinly sliced
1 small carrot, thinly sliced
$\frac{1}{4}$ green or red (bell) pepper,
  seeded and thinly sliced
1 large flour tortilla,
  about 20 cm/8 in

1 Make the filling the night before. Mix 5 ml/1 tsp of the oil with the paprika, lemon juice, yoghurt and salt and pepper to taste. Add the chicken and stir to coat in the mixture. Leave in a cool place to marinate for 30 minutes, if possible.

2 Heat the remaining oil in a frying pan. Add the onion, carrot and sliced pepper and cook gently for 5 minutes, stirring frequently. Add the marinated chicken mixture and continue to cook for 10–15 minutes until the vegetables are tender and the chicken cooked through.

3 Tip the filling into a bowl, allow to cool, then cover and chill overnight in the fridge.

4 The following day, spoon the filling on to the tortilla, placing it to one side of the centre. Wrap the unfilled half around the filling. Wrap in clingfilm (plastic wrap) and keep chilled until ready to pack.

Cans of spicy refried beans contain onion, red pepper, cumin and Jalapeño chillies, as well as crushed pinto beans. It's a fairly hot and spicy mixture so, if preferred, use just 15 ml/ 1 tbsp and spread it very thinly over the tortilla. The remaining beans can be kept in a covered bowl in the fridge for 2 days.

easy bean burritos with corn tortillas

MAKES 1

1 large corn tortilla,
about 20 cm/8 in
45 ml/3 tbsp canned spicy
refried beans

15 ml/1 tbsp soured (dairy sour)
cream or Greek-style yoghurt
50 g/2 oz/$^1/_2$ cup coarsely grated
Cheddar cheese
Shredded iceberg lettuce

1 Lay the tortilla on a board and spoon the beans along the centre. Drizzle the soured cream or yoghurt over, then pile with the grated cheese and some shredded lettuce.

2 Roll up the tortilla, tucking in the ends to make a parcel. Wrap in clingfilm (plastic wrap) and keep chilled until ready to pack.

Tortillas in the school lunchbox are such a far cry from the boring plain cheese 'doorsteps' of earlier generations! The tuna will benefit from a little salt, but remember that we should all be trying to reduce the amount of salt we eat so add it very sparingly. As well as being attractive, the tomatoes add flavour.

tuna and cherry tomato tortilla with tomato mayonnaise

MAKES 1

1 large flour tortilla, about
  20 cm/8 in
90 g/3½ oz/½ small can of tuna,
  drained and flaked
5 ml/1 tsp tomato ketchup (catsup)

10 ml/2 tsp mayonnaise
15 ml/1 tbsp Greek-style yoghurt
Salt and pepper (optional)
6 cherry tomatoes (red or yellow, or
  a mixture), quartered

1 Lay the tortilla on a board. Mash the tuna with the ketchup in a small bowl, then stir in the mayonnaise and yoghurt. Season with a little salt and pepper, if liked.

2 Spread the tuna mixture over the tortilla, then scatter with the cherry tomatoes.

3 Roll up the tortilla, tucking in the ends to make a parcel. Wrap in clingfilm (plastic wrap) and keep chilled until ready to pack.

This delicious wrap is ideal for a packed lunch as it will actually improve during the morning! The dried fruit will soften and become juicier by lunchtime as it soaks up some of the moisture from the ricotta. You can vary the fruits depending on your child's preferences and what is available.

dried fruit and nut ricotta pancake roll

MAKES 1

1 large sweet crêpe or thin pancake, about 20 cm/8 in
50 g/2 oz/¼ cup ricotta cheese
5 ml/1 tsp runny honey

50 g/2 oz/⅓ cup no-need-to-soak dried fruit such as apricots, dates or tropical fruits

1 Lay the pancake on a board. Mix together the ricotta and honey and spread over the pancake.

2 Chop or snip with kitchen scissors the dried fruit into smaller pieces, if necessary. Scatter over the ricotta.

3 Roll up the pancake, tucking in the ends to make a parcel. Wrap tightly in clingfilm (plastic wrap) and keep chilled until ready to pack.

Pittas make brilliant 'pockets' for substantial fillings. Add extra salad if liked, such as sliced cucumber, chopped celery or drained canned sweetcorn. If you prepare the filling the night before, keep the egg mayonnaise and bacon in separate covered dishes so that the bacon stays crisp.

egg and bacon pitta pocket with cress

MAKES 1

1 egg
15 ml/1 tbsp mayonnaise or salad cream
2 streaky or back bacon rashers (slices)

1 small round pitta bread, about 50 g/2 oz
Softened butter or margarine (optional)
Mustard and cress

1 Put the egg in a small pan of cold water. Bring to the boil, then lower the heat slightly so that the egg is boiling gently. Cook for 8 minutes, then drain and rinse under cold running water. Peel off the shell.

2 Roughly chop the egg, put in a bowl with the mayonnaise or salad cream and mix together. (There is no need to season with salt as the bacon will be salty already.)

3 Grill the bacon until well cooked and crispy. Cool, then crumble or snip into small pieces with kitchen scissors. Stir into the egg mixture.

4 Warm the pitta in the microwave for a few seconds, then cut 2 cm/³⁄₄ in off the top and open up to make a pocket. Thinly spread the inside with butter or margarine, if liked.

5 Spoon in the egg and bacon mixture and add some snipped mustard and cress. Wrap in clingfilm (plastic wrap) and keep chilled until ready to pack.

To reduce the saltiness of Feta cheese, rinse it in water, then leave it to soak in cold water for 10 minutes while preparing the other ingredients. Overnight marinating improves the flavour and draws out excess juices from the tomato and cucumber. If possible, warm the pitta first to make it easier to open up.

greek salad pitta pocket with cucumber

MAKES 1

15 ml/1 tbsp light olive oil
10 ml/2 tsp red wine vinegar
5 ml/1 tsp fresh chopped herbs
   such as parsley, or a tiny pinch of
   dried mixed herbs
1 ripe plum tomato
50 g/2 oz Feta cheese

2.5 cm/1 in piece of cucumber,
   quartered and sliced into chunks
2 stoned (pitted) black olives, thinly
   sliced (optional)
1 large oval plain or sesame pitta
   bread, about 65 g/2½ oz
Shredded lettuce (optional)

1 Make the filling the night before. Put the oil, vinegar and herbs in a bowl and whisk with a fork to mix.

2 Cut the tomato into wedges, then cut each wedge in half widthways. Cut the Feta into small cubes. Add these to the bowl with the cucumber and olives, if using, and toss together thoroughly. Cover and marinate in the fridge overnight.

3 The following day, tip the salad into a sieve (strainer) and drain off the excess liquid. Cut the pitta in half and carefully open out each half to make a pocket.

4 Put a little shredded lettuce in the bottom of each pitta pocket, if liked, then spoon in the Greek salad. Wrap in clingfilm (plastic wrap) and keep chilled until ready to pack.

Nutritional note

Parsley is an excellent source of vitamin C, iron and calcium. Try to encourage your child to enjoy this fresh herb from an early age.

These Middle Eastern bean patties are traditionally deep-fried; in my healthier version the falafels are baked until crisp. The mixture can be made, shaped and kept chilled for up to 24 hours. They are delicious served with tzatziki or a Greek yoghurt dressing with chopped fresh coriander or mint.

falafel pitta
with lettuce and tomato

MAKES 2

100 g/4 oz canned chickpeas
(garbanzos), drained and rinsed
5 ml/1 tsp olive oil
A small pinch of ground cumin
A small pinch of ground turmeric
1 small garlic clove, crushed
(optional)
5 ml/1 tsp lemon juice

½ small carrot, finely grated
Salt and pepper
1 large oval sesame pitta bread,
about 65 g/2½ oz
Softened butter or margarine
(optional)
Shredded lettuce
3 baby plum tomatoes, quartered

1 Put the chickpeas in a small bowl with the oil and crush them with a fork until the mixture is smooth. Stir in the spices, the garlic, if using, lemon juice and carrot. Season with salt and pepper to taste, then mix well. Alternatively, if your food processor is suitable for small quantities, blend the ingredients except the carrot together, then stir in the carrot.

2 Shape the mixture into four flat, round patties, each about 3 cm/ 1¼ in across. Place on a baking (cookie) sheet lined with non-stick baking parchment and bake in a preheated oven at 200°C/ 400°F/gas 6/fan oven 180°C for 15–20 minutes or until lightly browned, turning them over half-way through the cooking time. Allow the falafel to cool, then keep covered in the fridge until ready to use.

3 In the morning, warm the pitta in a microwave for a few seconds to make it easy to open (if you don't have a microwave, warm it in the oven for 2–3 minutes after baking the falafels, then split open, cool and keep in a plastic bag overnight). Cut the pitta in half and carefully open out each half to make a pocket.

4 If liked, thinly butter the inside of the pitta. Fill each half with two falafels, shredded lettuce and the tomatoes. Wrap each half in clingfilm (plastic wrap) and keep chilled until ready to pack.

Nutritional note

Chickpeas are an excellent source of protein and also contain plenty of iron – essential in children's diets.

The choice of breads and rolls in the supermarkets is enormous, making it easy to add variety to packed lunches. This combination is delicious in a big floury bap, but may be too much of a mouthful for smaller children. For them, cut and butter long bread rolls, such as mini baguettes or soft hot dog rolls.

big brunch
sausage bap

MAKES 1

1 egg
15 ml/1 tbsp mayonnaise
5 ml/1 tsp wholegrain mustard or chutney
Salt and pepper (optional)

1 cold grilled (broiled) or fried sausage
1 plum tomato
1 soft or crusty white bap
Softened butter or margarine

1   Put the egg in a small saucepan of cold water and bring to the boil. Lower the heat and simmer for 8 minutes. Drain the egg and cool in a bowl of cold water (this will stop a black ring forming around the yolk). Peel off the shell and cut the egg into slices.

2   Mix together the mayonnaise and mustard or chutney, adding a little salt and pepper if liked. Slice the sausage lengthwise so that it will lie flat, making the roll easier to eat. Slice the tomato.

3   Split the roll in half and thinly spread with butter or margarine. Arrange the sliced sausage on the bottom half, spread half the flavoured mayonnaise over, then top with the tomato slices. Dab with the remaining mayonnaise, then top with the sliced egg. Replace the top half of the bap. Cut in half for easier-eating, wrap in clingfilm (plastic wrap) and keep chilled until ready to pack.

Soft submarine rolls are usually massive, about 18 cm/7 in long, so are ideal for big appetites. You can also buy tiny mini subs, which are more suitable for younger children. The prawn and crabmeat mixtures may be made the night before, in which case you may find it quicker and easier to make it as one filling.

seafood sub
with tomato mayonnaise

MAKES 1

¹/₂ x 120 g/4¹/₂ oz/small can of white
  crabmeat, well drained
30 ml/2 tbsp mayonnaise
  or 15 ml/1 tbsp each mayonnaise
  and Greek-style yoghurt
1 cornichon, chopped or sliced

1 large submarine roll
Softened butter or margarine
A few little gem lettuce leaves
2.5 ml/¹/₂ tsp tomato purée (paste)
50 g/2 oz cooked, peeled prawns
  (shrimp), thawed if frozen

1 Put the crabmeat in a small bowl with half the mayonnaise or mayonnaise and yoghurt. Add the cornichon and mix together.

2 Using a sharp knife, split the sub open lengthways, keeping it still attached along one side like a hinge. Thinly butter both sides. Tear the lettuce leaves into smaller pieces and use half to line one side of the roll. Spoon the crabmeat over the lettuce.

3 Place the remaining mayonnaise or mayonnaise and yoghurt in the bowl. Blend in the tomato purée, then add the prawns and mix well.

4 Spoon the prawns on top of the crabmeat, then top with the remaining lettuce. Close the roll, cut it in half for easier eating, then wrap in clingfilm (plastic wrap) and keep chilled until ready to pack.

Nutritional note

Crab is an excellent source of phosphorus, a mineral needed for the development of healthy bones.

Ciabatta comes from northern Italy and has a floury crust, a moist open texture and a subtle olive oil taste. Chorizo is a spicy Spanish sausage and can be bought whole or sliced in small quantities from the deli counter. With this moist, well-flavoured filling, there's no need to butter the roll.

little italy ciabatta
with mozzarella

MAKES 1

5 ml/1 tsp olive oil
A few drops of balsamic or red wine
   vinegar
¼ red or yellow (bell) pepper, very
   thinly sliced
1 ciabatta roll

25 g/1 oz Mozzarella cheese, thinly
   sliced
10 ml/2 tsp tomato relish
3 slices of chorizo sausage, thinly
   sliced, or 1 mini pepperami stick,
   sliced
Shredded iceberg lettuce

1 Put the oil and vinegar in a bowl, add the sliced pepper and toss to coat. Set aside.

2 Using a serrated knife, cut the ciabatta almost in half horizontally so that it is still 'hinged' when you open it up.

3 Arrange the Mozzarella on the bottom half of the roll, then spoon the tomato relish over. Top with the chorizo, followed by the pepper slices and some shredded lettuce. Close the roll and wrap in clingfilm (plastic wrap). Keep chilled until ready to pack.

Nutritional note

Chorizo has a high fat content so, if you prefer, it can be reduced by first frying the slices in a dry pan, then patting dry on kitchen paper (paper towels).

A buttery brioche is delicious filled with really crispy streaky bacon. You can either prepare this at home or buy it ready-cooked from the supermarket. The bacon will loose its crispness if it touches moist ingredients, so here the brioche is cut into three layers to keep the different fillings apart.

crispy bacon
brioche fingers

MAKES 1

2 streaky bacon rashers (slices)	A few little gem lettuce leaves, torn
1 brioche finger roll	10 ml/2 tsp mayonnaise, salad
Softened butter or margarine	cream or relish

1 Cut the rind off the bacon rashers and grill (broil) or fry until well cooked and crispy. Drain on kitchen paper (paper towels).

2 Cut the brioche lengthways into three layers and thinly butter on all the cut sides. Place the bottom part of the roll on a board and top with some torn lettuce, then dab with mayonnaise, salad cream or relish. Top with the middle section of the roll.

3 Place the bacon on the middle slice, then finish by replacing the top of the roll. Wrap in clingfilm (plastic wrap) and keep chilled until ready to pack.

Large crusty rolls can be hollowed out and filled for a lunchtime surprise. This mildly spicy chicken mixture can be made the night before and will keep for 2–3 days in the fridge, so there's enough here for two servings. Save the bread scooped out of the roll and use it for making breadcrumbs.

chicken and sweetcorn roll with mango

MAKES 1

10 ml/2 tsp sunflower oil
½ small onion, very finely chopped
1 small clove garlic, crushed
2.5 ml/½ tsp mild curry powder
15 ml/1 tbsp mango chutney
5 ml/1 tsp lemon juice
5 ml/1 tsp tomato purée (paste)
100 ml/3½ fl oz/scant ½ cup Greek-style yoghurt

1 cooked chicken breast, cut into bite-sized pieces
30 ml/2 tbsp canned sweetcorn, drained (optional)
1 large domed crusty white bread roll, about 10 cm/4 in across
Softened butter or margarine

1   Heat the oil in a small frying pan, add the onion and cook gently for 5 minutes, stirring frequently, until softened. Add the garlic and curry powder and cook for a further 1 minute, stirring all the time. Remove the pan from the heat, tip the mixture into a bowl and stir in the chutney, lemon juice and tomato purée. Leave to cool.

2   Stir in the yoghurt, followed by the chicken and sweetcorn, if using.

3   Slice off the top the bread roll and set aside. Scoop out most of the soft interior, leaving a 'shell' about 2 cm/¾ in thick. Lightly butter the cut side of the lid and the inside of the roll. Spoon half the chicken mixture into the hollow, then replace the lid. Wrap in clingfilm (plastic wrap) and keep chilled until ready to pack.

Tip

Serve the second portion with rice as a salad or use it for a sandwich or wrap filling. Add some fruit to the mixture just before using, if liked: halved small seedless grapes or chopped dried fruit all work well.

Pan bagna is a classic layered sandwich from southern France. It's ideal for packed lunches and picnics as it benefits from being made several hours in advance so that the flavours can mingle and the juices soak into the bread a little. Traditionally it uses anchovies, but this recipe with tuna is more child-friendly.

egg, tuna and tomato pan bagna

MAKES 1

1 egg
1 large baguette roll or an 18 cm/
 7 in slice from a baguette loaf
90 g/3½ oz/½ small can of tuna in
 olive or sunflower oil
2.5 ml/½ tsp red wine vinegar

A small pinch of caster (superfine)
 sugar
1 tomato
15 ml/1 tbsp mayonnaise
Salt and pepper (optional)

1 Put the egg in a small saucepan of cold water and bring to the boil. Lower the heat and simmer for 8 minutes, then drain and rinse under cold running water. Peel and slice.

2 Using a sharp knife, split the bread open lengthways, keeping it still attached along one side like a hinge. Drain the tuna, reserving 10 ml/2 tsp of the oil. Put the oil in a small bowl with the vinegar and sugar and whisk with a fork.

3 Slice the tomato, then cut each slice in half. Add to the vinaigrette mixture and toss well. Flake the tuna, then mix with the mayonnaise and a little salt and pepper, if liked. Spoon and spread this over the bottom half of the baguette.

4 Layer up the egg and tomato slices over the tuna. Close up the roll, cut it in half for easier eating, then wrap in clingfilm (plastic wrap) and keep chilled until ready to pack.

Tip

Avoid crusty or chewy bread for children with wobbly teeth, or those who wear braces.

---

*It seems as though all children like pizza, and now yours can
have them for school lunch. Split muffins make great mini
bases, or you could use a hamburger bun if you prefer. Try
other topping combinations such as tuna and sweetcorn,
Cheddar and cherry tomato, or red pepper and peperoni.*

ham and pineapple
pizza muffin

MAKES ONE SERVING OF 2 PIZZAS

1 white or wholemeal English
   muffin, sliced in half horizontally
10 ml/2 tsp tomato purée (paste)
2.5 ml/½ tsp olive oil
A tiny pinch of dried mixed herbs

1 slice of ham, cut into strips
1 canned pineapple ring, chopped
40 g/1½ oz Mozzarella cheese, cut
   into thin strips

1 Preheat the grill (broiler) to high. Place the muffin halves, cut-side down, on the grill rack and cook for 1–2 minutes until the bases are lightly toasted, then turn the muffins over. Grill (broil) until they are just golden.

2 Mix together the tomato purée, oil and herbs and spread half over the cut side of each toasted muffin. Lay the ham strips on top, roughly parallel to each other. Scatter with the pineapple pieces.

3 Arrange the Mozzarella strips on top at right-angles to the ham (this will help the topping stay in place). Cook under the hot grill for 3–4 minutes or until the cheese has melted and is lightly browned in places. Remove from the grill and allow to cool.

4 When completely cold, wrap the pizzas in foil or clingfilm (plastic wrap) and keep chilled until ready to pack.

SALADS
AND DIPS

Sandwiches may be the mainstay of packed lunches, but there are many other options to liven up your child's lunchbox. Salads are a delicious way to enjoy a wide variety of foods and have come a long way since the obligatory limp lettuce leaf, sliced tomato and dollop of salad cream. Deliciously fresh salads can be prepared from all kinds of fruit and vegetables, along with starchy carbohydrates such as rice, pasta and bulghar wheat. These are a great way to help achieve the target of eating at least five portions of fruit and vegetables a day.

Most children love dips and you'll find plenty of quick and easy ideas here, including a creamy cheese dip and a lighter and healthier hummus. These can be served with bought dippers such as breadsticks or you can make your own vegetable crisps or low-fat tortilla chips.

This delicious crunchy salad will keep well for up to 2 days. If liked, use the second portion the following day to fill a crusty mini baguette lined with lettuce. To ring the changes, you could vary the second portion by adding a few halved seedless black or green grapes and chopped pecans or walnuts.

shredded chicken with lemon coleslaw

MAKES 2 PORTIONS

1 red dessert (eating) apple
15 ml/1 tbsp lemon juice
1 stick of celery, trimmed and finely chopped
2 spring onions (scallions), trimmed and thinly sliced

50 g/2 oz red or white cabbage, very finely shredded
45 ml/3 tbsp mayonnaise
1 large roasted chicken breast, skinned
5 ml/1 tsp toasted sesame seeds
Salt and pepper

1 Quarter the apple and remove the core, but do not peel. Coarsely grate into the bowl, add the lemon juice and toss.

2 Add the celery, spring onions, cabbage and mayonnaise and mix until all the ingredients are thoroughly coated.

3 Shred the chicken breast and add with the sesame seeds. Season with salt and pepper and mix again. Spoon the salad into two separate containers and keep chilled until ready to pack.

The classic Salade Niçoise from southern France includes anchovies and whole green beans; this simplified version is equally delicious, but is a more child-friendly introduction to this dish. Try to get the whole family into the healthy habit of eating omega-3-rich oily fish such as tuna, sardines and salmon.

niçoise-style luncheon salad

MAKES 1 PORTION

1 small or medium egg
Up to 1.5 ml/¼ tsp Dijon mustard
15 ml/1 tbsp olive oil
5 ml/1 tsp white wine vinegar
A tiny pinch of caster (superfine) sugar
Salt and pepper (optional)

90 g/3½ oz/½ small can of tuna, drained
4 cherry tomatoes
50 g/2 oz cooked new potatoes, cut into 1 cm/½ in cubes
¼ little gem lettuce, shredded
2 stoned (pitted) black olives, quartered or sliced (optional)

1 Put the egg in a small saucepan of cold water and bring to a gentle boil. Lower the heat and simmer for 8 minutes. Drain the egg and cool in a bowl of cold water (this will stop a black ring forming around the yolk). Peel off the shell, cut the egg in half widthways, then each half into four chunks.

2 Put the mustard, oil, vinegar and sugar in a mixing bowl and whisk together with a fork. Add a little salt and pepper if liked.

3 Roughly flake the tuna and cut the tomatoes into quarters. Add the tuna, tomatoes and potato cubes to the dressing and gently mix together.

4 Put the shredded lettuce into the serving container. Spoon the potato, tuna and tomato mixture over the lettuce, then top with the pieces of egg. Scatter with the olives, if using. Put the lid on the container and keep chilled in the fridge until ready to pack.

Tabbouleh is a classic Middle Eastern salad made with bulghar – coarsely ground wheat grains that have been parboiled. It takes 10 minutes to cook, giving you plenty of time to prepare the rest of the salad. A few toasted pine nuts would give additional protein.

tabbouleh
with feta cheese

MAKES 2 PORTIONS

100 g/4 oz/1 cup bulghar (cracked wheat)
300 ml/¹/₂ pint/1¹/₄ cups boiling vegetable stock or water
¹/₂ red or yellow (bell) pepper, seeded and thinly sliced
2 spring onions (scallions), sliced
5 cm/2 in piece of cucumber, chopped
1 carrot, grated
8 cherry tomatoes, quartered

30 ml/2 tbsp chopped fresh parsley
15 ml/1 tbsp chopped fresh coriander (cilantro) or mint (optional)
100 g/4 oz Feta cheese
30 ml/2 tbsp light olive or sunflower oil
10 ml/2 tsp red or white wine vinegar
A pinch of caster (superfine) sugar

1 Check the cooking instructions on the packet of bulghar; some varieties simply need soaking rather than simmering in boiling water. Depending on the instructions, put the bulghar in a small saucepan and pour over the stock or water. Bring back to the boil, reduce the heat, cover and simmer for 5 minutes. Uncover and continue cooking, stirring occasionally, for 3–4 minutes or until the bulghar is tender and all the liquid has been absorbed.

2 When the bulghar is cool, add the pepper slices, onions, cucumber, carrot, tomatoes and herbs and gently mix together.

3 Briefly soak the Feta in cold water to remove some of the saltiness. Pat it dry on kitchen paper (paper towels), then crumble it into small pieces.

4 Using a fork, whisk together the oil, vinegar and sugar in a small bowl. Drizzle over the salad and gently mix again. Divide between two airtight containers. Sprinkle half of the cheese over each one, then put the lids on the containers and chill in the fridge until ready to pack.

Nutritional note

Bulghar is a good source of starchy carbohydrate, which is great for prolonged energy.

Here, marinated strips of chicken are grilled, then served with rice and crunchy shredded vegetables and drizzled with a peanut dressing. If you've made a Chinese stir-fry the night before, you may have some of these ingredients to hand. Don't add any salt because the soy sauce already has plenty.

chicken satay salad
with peanut dressing

MAKES 2 PORTIONS

FOR THE SALAD:
1 large boneless chicken breast, skinned
20 ml/4 tsp sunflower oil
15 ml/1 tbsp soy sauce
1 small garlic clove, crushed
2 cm/³/₄ in piece of fresh root ginger, peeled and grated, or 1.5 ml/¹/₄ tsp ground ginger
100 g/4 oz/¹/₂ cup easy-cook white or basmati rice
10 ml/2 tsp lime or lemon juice

¹/₄ small head of Chinese leaves (stem lettuce), about 100 g/4 oz, very finely shredded
¹/₄ cucumber, diced

FOR THE PEANUT DRESSING:
25 g/1 oz creamed coconut, roughly chopped
75 ml/5 tbsp boiling water
30 ml/2 tbsp crunchy peanut butter
10 ml/2 tsp soy sauce
2.5 ml/¹/₂ tsp soft light brown sugar

1 To make the salad, cut the chicken into long strips about 1 cm/¹/₂ in wide. Mix together 10 ml/2 tsp of the oil, the soy sauce, garlic and ginger. Add the chicken, mix well to coat and leave to marinate while preparing the remaining ingredients (or leave for several hours in the fridge if preferred).

2 Rinse the rice in a sieve (strainer) under cold running water, then tip into a saucepan. Add plenty of boiling water and bring back to the boil. Reduce the heat and simmer for 10 minutes or according to the packet instructions until tender. Drain in the sieve and rinse with cold water. Drain again.

3 Remove the chicken from the marinade and thread the strips on to skewers. Grill (broil) under a preheated grill (broiler) for 8–10 minutes, turning occasionally and brushing with the marinade for the first 5 minutes. Take the chicken off the skewers and leave to cool.

4 Whisk together the remaining oil and the lime or lemon juice in a mixing bowl with a fork. Add the rice, Chinese leaves and cucumber and mix well.

5 To make the peanut dressing, blend the coconut with the boiling water in a small jug. Whisk in all the remaining ingredients. Leave until completely cool.

6 Divide the rice mixture between two containers. Top with the grilled chicken strips and drizzle with the dressing. Put on the lids and keep chilled until ready to pack.

Tip

You can use leftover cooked rice for this dish, rather than cooking fresh. Cooked rice should always be kept cool to prevent the possibility of food poisoning. Cool it as quickly as possible (spreading it out on a chilled plate helps), then keep in a covered container in the fridge for no more than 2 days. For longer keeping, rice freezes well.

Here, raisins or sultanas soaked in honey and citrus juices, sweet grated carrot, mild Dutch cheese and crunchy croûtons are combined to make a delicious yet simple salad. Carrots are a valuable source of beta-carotene, an antioxidant that boosts the body's ability to fight bacterial and viral infections.

dutch cheese and carrot salad

MAKES 1 PORTION

15 ml/1 tbsp orange juice
5 ml/1 tsp lemon juice
15 ml/1 tbsp sunflower oil
2.5 ml/½ tsp clear honey
Salt and pepper (optional)

15 ml/1 tbsp raisins or sultanas
  (golden raisins)
1 slice of white or brown bread
1 carrot, peeled
40 g/1½ oz Gouda or Edam (Dutch)
  cheese

1 Put the fruit juices, 5 ml/1 tsp of the oil and the honey in a mixing bowl and whisk together with a fork, adding a little salt and pepper, if liked. Stir in the raisins or sultanas to coat in the dressing, then leave to soak while preparing the other ingredients.

2 Cut the bread into small cubes. Heat the remaining oil in a frying pan, add the bread and fry, turning frequently, until crisp and golden all over. Drain on kitchen paper (paper towels) and leave to cool.

3 Coarsely grate the carrot and add to the raisins. Mix well and spoon into a small container. Cut the cheese into thin strips and scatter on top of the salad. Cover with a lid and keep chilled until ready to pack. Put the croûtons in a small plastic bag or container and pack separately, ready to scatter over the salad.

Couscous is a mixture of semolina flour and water rolled in flour to produce tiny yellow grains. Make sure you choose a brand that only needs soaking rather than lengthy steaming. Add extra protein to this dish by scattering with chopped egg, cubes of ham or chicken or some grated cheese.

middle eastern spicy couscous

MAKES 1 PORTION

15 ml/1 tbsp pine nuts
15 ml/1 tbsp light olive or sunflower oil
2 spring onions (scallions), chopped
1/2 garlic clove, crushed (optional)
A pinch of ground cumin
120 ml/4 fl oz/1/2 cup vegetable stock

10 ml/2 tsp lemon juice
50 g/2 oz/1/3 cup couscous
2 tomatoes, peeled and chopped
2 cm/3/4 in piece of cucumber, finely diced
15 ml/1 tbsp chopped fresh parsley
Salt and pepper (optional)

1 Put the pine nuts in a small non-stick pan and cook them over a gentle heat, stirring frequently, until just golden. Tip on to a small plate and leave to cool.

2 Add 5 ml/1 tsp of the oil to the frying pan, add the spring onions and garlic and cook gently for 2 minutes until soft. Stir in the cumin and cook for a few seconds more.

3 Pour in the stock, the remaining oil and the lemon juice and bring to the boil. Turn off the heat, then add the couscous, stir briefly and cover the pan with a lid. Leave for 5 minutes or until the couscous has absorbed all the liquid. Tip the mixture into a bowl, stir with a fork to separate the grains and leave to cool.

4 Add all the remaining ingredients to the bowl and season with salt and pepper, if liked. Spoon into a suitable container and keep chilled until ready to pack.

Pasta comes in a huge variety of colours and shapes – spirals, bows and shells are just a few. You can sometimes even find radiatore pasta, which looks like tiny radiators! Let your child help you choose when you next go to the supermarket. Flaked canned tuna or salmon makes a good alternative to the prawns.

prawn and courgette pasta salad

MAKES 1 PORTION

25 g/1 oz small pasta shapes
¹/₂ small courgette (zucchini), cut into 5 mm/¹/₄ in slices
15 ml/1 tbsp mayonnaise
15 ml/1 tbsp natural yoghurt
2.5 ml/¹/₂ tsp tomato purée (paste)

Salt and pepper (optional)
¹/₄ small red or yellow (bell) pepper, finely diced
50 g/2 oz cooked, peeled prawns (shrimp), thawed if frozen

1 Cook the pasta in boiling lightly salted water according to the packet instructions until just tender, adding the courgette slices to the pan for the last 2 minutes of cooking time. Drain and rinse briefly under cold water to cool. Drain well.

2 Blend together the mayonnaise, yoghurt and tomato purée in a bowl, seasoning with a little salt and pepper, if liked.

3 Add the cooled pasta mixture, the diced pepper and the prawns to the mayonnaise mixture and gently mix together. Spoon into a suitable container and keep chilled until ready to pack.

This colourful crunchy salad has a sweet and sour dressing that young children often find appealing. If you're serving it as the main part of the packed lunch, rather than as an accompaniment, add some strips of cooked chicken breast for protein. Instructions for sprouting your own beans are on page 72.

crunchy oriental salad

MAKES 1 PORTION

FOR THE SALAD:
1 small carrot
½ stick of celery
½ crisp red eating (dessert) apple
40 g/1½ oz beansprouts such as
   mung beans or alfalfa seeds

FOR THE DRESSING:
5 ml/1 tsp sunflower oil
2.5 ml/½ tsp sesame oil or extra
   sunflower oil
5 ml/1 tsp honey
5 ml/1 tsp red wine vinegar

1 To make the salad, cut the carrot into 4 cm/1½ in lengths. Slice them thinly lengthways, then cut into very fine matchsticks. Thinly slice the celery or cut into pieces the same size as the carrot. Cut the apple into eight wedges, remove the core, then cut across into thin slices.

2 Combine the carrot, celery, apple and beansprouts in a bowl.

3 To make the dressing, whisk together all the ingredients in a small bowl with a fork.

4 Drizzle the dressing over the salad and toss gently to coat. Spoon into a suitable container and keep chilled until ready to pack.

When you want to pack something that's both fun to eat and nutritious, dips and dippers make a great choice. Ring the changes by using different cheeses in this dip; Red Leicester works well or, if your child is a fan of blue cheese, try a creamy Stilton, crumbled then mashed with the soft cheese until smooth.

smooth and creamy double cheese dip

MAKES 2 PORTIONS

50 g/2 oz/¼ cup full-fat soft cream cheese
15 ml/1 tbsp soured (dairy sour) cream or Greek-style yoghurt

50 g/2 oz/½ cup cheese such as mild Cheddar, finely grated
Salt and pepper (optional)

1 Beat the cream cheese until soft, then beat in the soured cream or yoghurt. Stir in the grated cheese and season to taste with salt and pepper, if liked.

2 Spoon into two small containers and keep chilled until ready to pack. Store in the fridge for up to 2 days.

Serving tip

The dip is good served with mini breadsticks, low-fat tortilla chips or vegetable crudités.

This dip, like all the ones in this chapter, is quick and easy to make and is much less expensive than ready-made varieties. It's a light-textured, refreshing dip, perfect for hot weather, when your child will want something cool to eat. Serve with lots of vegetable crudités (see page 70) and breadsticks.

butter bean, cottage cheese and watercress dip

MAKES 2 PORTIONS

200 g/7 oz/1 small can of butter (lima) beans, rinsed and drained
100 g/4 oz/¹/₂ cup cottage cheese
30 ml/2 tbsp mayonnaise

25 g/1 oz watercress, roughly chopped
15 ml/1 tbsp parsley, roughly chopped
Salt (optional)

1 Put the beans, cheese and mayonnaise in a food processor and blend for a few seconds.

2 Add the watercress and parsley and blend again until the mixture is fairly smooth. Season to taste with a little salt, if liked.

3 Divide between two containers and keep chilled until ready to pack. Store in the fridge for up to 2 days.

Nutritional note

Watercress is packed with vitamins and minerals, especially vitamins C, E and beta-carotene, all of which are powerful antioxidants.

Hummus is so simple to make, and this is lower in fat than most shop-bought varieties. As well as a dip, it's good spread in tortilla wraps and with shredded salad in pitta breads. Chickpeas are a good source of iron, which helps prevent anaemia, a common nutritional problem in teenage girls.

hummus

MAKES 2 GENEROUS PORTIONS

½ x 400 g/14 oz/large can of
   chickpeas (garbanzos), drained
   and rinsed
75 ml/5 tbsp fromage frais
15 ml/1 tbsp olive oil

15 ml/1 tbsp lemon juice
A pinch of ground cumin
1 small garlic clove, crushed
Salt and pepper (optional)

1 Put all the ingredients except the seasoning in a food processor and blend for 2–3 minutes until very smooth, stopping and scraping down the sides half-way through. Season, if liked, with salt and pepper.

2 Divide between two airtight containers and keep chilled until ready to pack.

This dip really couldn't be quicker or easier to make. Tinned crab is a great storecupboard standby and goes well with crunchy vegetable crudités (see page 70). Drain the crabmeat in a sieve, then squeeze it dry with your hands. Crabmeat is usually canned in brine, so there's no need to season this dip.

simple tangy crabmeat dip

MAKES 2 GENEROUS PORTIONS

30 ml/2 tbsp mayonnaise
2.5 ml/½ tsp tomato purée (paste)
5 ml/1 tsp lemon juice

120 g/5 oz/1 small can of white crabmeat, thoroughly drained
1–2 cornichons, very finely chopped

1 Blend together the mayonnaise, tomato purée and lemon juice in a small bowl.

2 Stir in the crabmeat and cornichons.

3 Divide between two airtight containers and keep chilled until ready to pack.

vegetable crudités

Lots of vegetables can be used to make crudités. Try to include at least two different types your child enjoys and match them to the dip.

1 Cut carrots, cucumber and celery into chunky sticks, and seeded red and yellow (bell) peppers into strips.

2 You could also include a few thoroughly washed whole button mushrooms, and florets of broccoli, cauliflower or calabrese.

3 Don't overdo the quantity, as raw vegetables are filling and time-consuming to eat.

4 Include a few small breadsticks as well to vary the texture.

crispy pitta strips

Make your own crispy pitta strips for nibbling and dipping!

1 Lightly brush one side of a mini wholemeal or plain pitta bread with olive oil. Sprinkle with 5 ml/1 tsp of sesame seeds and cook under a hot grill (broiler) for about 1 minute or until the bread and seeds are golden.

2 Turn over, brush the other side of the pitta with oil and sprinkle again with sesame seeds. Return to the hot grill and cook for a further 1 minute.

3 Using kitchen scissors, cut the warm pitta widthways into 2 cm/ $^3/_4$ in fingers. Leave to cool.

4 When completely cold, wrap tightly in clingfilm (plastic wrap) or foil to keep them crisp.

Serving tip

These go especially well with Hummus (see page 68) and taramasalata.

---

vegetable crisps

These are a healthy and tasty alternative to packet potato crisps. Make them when you're cooking and have a spare shelf in the oven.

1   Cut a medium-sized potato and a fat carrot into very thin slices, about 3 mm/$\frac{1}{8}$ in (use a mandolin or food processor attachment for this, if possible). Put them in a bowl and drizzle with 15 ml/ 1 tbsp of sunflower or light olive oil, then toss them until all the slices are lightly coated.

2   Place them in a single layer on a non-stick baking (cookie) sheet (or a baking sheet lined with non-stick baking parchment). Sprinkle with a little salt, if liked.

3   Bake in a preheated oven at 200°C/400°F/gas 6/fan oven 180°C for 30–40 minutes, turning them over once or twice, until crisp and golden, checking frequently towards the end of the cooking time to make sure they do not burn. Transfer to a wire cooling rack and leave to cool.

tortilla chips

Bought tortilla chips are incredibly high in fat and salt and are often flavoured with strong spices and garlic, which may make your child an unpopular classroom partner! These are a lower-fat alternative.

1   Lightly brush a large corn tortilla with 5 ml/1 tsp of light olive oil, then cut into wedges with kitchen scissors.

2   Spread them out on a large baking (cookie) sheet and bake in a preheated oven at 160°C/325°F/gas 3/fan oven 145°C for 15 minutes or until crisp and firm.

3   Transfer to a wire cooling rack and leave to cool.

Bean sprouts add crunch to salads and sandwiches. While they're easily available in supermarkets, it's fun for children to grow their own. Mung and aduki beansprouts are the ones usually sold, but whole green lentils, alfalfa seeds and chickpeas (garbanzos) also sprout well.

sprouting beans
for salads and sandwiches

1 Put a handful of dried pulses in a sieve (strainer) and rinse under running water. Put them in a large jar and half fill it with cold water. Cover with a piece of muslin secured with an elastic band. Leave to soak overnight.

2 The following day, pour off the water through the muslin, then refill the jar with water, again through the muslin. Shake gently, then drain off the water and place the jar on its side, away from direct sunlight.

3 Twice daily, rinse the pulses with fresh water and drain as above. After 2–4 days (depending on the variety of bean), they will begin to sprout.

4 When the shoots are at least 1 cm/½ in long, place the jar, still on its side, in a light or sunny (but not too hot) place. Leave for a further 2–3 days, rinsing and draining as before, until they have grown to the desired size (and before the leaves form).

5 Thoroughly rinse the sprouted beans, remove any that haven't germinated and keep in a plastic bag in the fridge for up to 2 days.

Nutritional note

Beansprouts contain useful amounts of vitamins B and C.

SUPER
SAVOURIES

Here you'll find a huge choice of savoury recipes, such as Sweet and Sticky Chicken Skewers and Mini Meatballs with Minted Yoghurt Dip. These can be prepared in advance, then quickly packed with a buttered bread roll or some crispbread the following morning. Others, including Spiced Turkey and Vegetable Calzone and Mixed Vegetable Filo Parcels are the main component of a packed lunch and need no other accompaniments.

There's also a selection of spreads and pâtés, both meat-based and vegetarian, that can be used as sandwich fillers or cut into slices and served with salads. In cooler weather, a flask of hot soup is a warming and welcome lunchtime treat; the recipes in this chapter make several portions, so that you can freeze some for another day.

These are based on yakitori, a popular Japanese dish. Shoyu is Japanese soy sauce with a subtler flavour than Chinese soy sauce. If you're using wooden skewers, soak them in cold water for 15 minutes before use to prevent them burning and to help keep the chicken moist.

sweet and sticky chicken skewers

MAKES 1 PORTION

About 1 cm/½ in piece of fresh root ginger
15 ml/1 tbsp shoyu or light soy sauce

5 ml/1 tsp white wine vinegar
10 ml/2 tsp light soft brown sugar
1 boneless chicken breast, skinned

1 Peel and grate the ginger, then squeeze out the juices into a small bowl. Add the shoyu or soy sauce, vinegar and sugar and whisk together with a fork.

2 Trim the chicken and cut it into bite-sized pieces. Add to the marinade and stir well to coat. Cover and leave to marinate in the fridge for at least 1 hour.

3 When ready to cook, thread the chicken on to one or two skewers, leaving a small gap between each piece. Cook under a preheated moderate grill (broiler) for 10–12 minutes, turning frequently and brushing with the marinade for only the first few minutes (because it contains raw chicken juices), until the chicken is thoroughly cooked.

4 When cool enough to handle, remove the chicken from the skewers. When completely cold, pack them in a small container. Don't forget to pack a fork for easy eating!

Nutritional note

Don't season these with extra salt, as there's already plenty in the shoyu or soy sauce.

Because they are so easy to eat, drumsticks are great for packed lunches and you can easily bake them when you're already using the oven. If you freeze the drumsticks, allow them to defrost in the fridge overnight before packing, and wrapping the ends in foil stops fingers getting too sticky.

honey-glazed chicken drumsticks

MAKES 4 PORTIONS

4 chicken drumsticks
30 ml/2 tbsp tomato ketchup (catsup)
15 ml/1 tbsp clear honey or maple syrup

10 ml/2 tsp sunflower oil
10 ml/2 tsp lemon juice
5 ml/1 tsp Worcestershire sauce

1 Wipe the chicken drumsticks with kitchen paper (paper towels). Using a sharp knife, cut two or three deep slashes through the skin and flesh of each.

2 Put all the remaining ingredients in a bowl and whisk together with a fork. Generously brush the drumsticks with the marinade. If time allows, leave to marinate in the fridge for several hours.

3 Place the drumsticks on a baking (cookie) sheet and cover loosely with foil. Bake in a preheated oven at 200°C/400°F/gas 6/fan oven 180°C for 20 minutes. Remove the foil, baste the chicken with the juices, then return to the oven for a further 10 minutes or until the juices run clear when the chicken is pierced with a skewer.

4 Allow the drumsticks to cool completely. Wrap a small piece of foil around the end of each to act as a handle, then wrap individually in non-stick baking parchment, then foil. They will keep in the fridge for up to 2 days.

*These can be served hot as part of a main meal or for party
food. If you don't want to use them all, open-freeze the sausage
nuggets, then pack in individual portions in freezer bags or
containers for up to 2 months. Allow them to defrost in the
fridge overnight before packing.*

crispy-coated
sausage nuggets

MAKES 20 SMALL NUGGETS (ABOUT 4 PORTIONS)

225 g/8 oz reduced-fat or premium
  sausagemeat
5 ml/1 tsp tomato purée (paste)
5 ml/1 tsp Worcestershire sauce
A pinch of dried mixed herbs

Salt and pepper
10 ml/2 tsp plain (all-purpose) flour
30 ml/2 tbsp sesame seeds
15 ml/1 tbsp sunflower or light olive
  oil

1 Put the sausagement in a bowl with the tomato purée,
Worcestershire sauce, herbs and a little salt and pepper. Using
your hands, mix together thoroughly.

2 Mix together the flour and sesame seeds on a small plate. Shape the
sausagemeat mixture into 20 small balls (keep them small so the
centres will be cooked by the time the sesame seeds have browned),
then roll a few at a time in the seed mixture to coat lightly.

3 Heat the oil in a large frying pan and cook the sausage nuggets in
two batches, turning frequently, until dark golden-brown and
crisp, adding a little more oil to the pan if necessary. The easiest
way to check that the nuggets are cooked is to remove one from
the pan and cut it open; there should be no sign of pinkness inside.

4 Drain the nuggets well on kitchen paper (paper towels) and leave
them to cool completely. Put a portion in a suitable container and
keep chilled until ready to pack.

Nutritional note

Pork is a good source of zinc and B vitamins, particularly
niacin and B12.

These moist meatballs are delicious served with a simple yoghurt dip. If you prefer, send them with a sachet or tiny carton of tomato ketchup or barbecue sauce instead. You can open-freeze the meatballs and pack them in portions in freezer bags or containers for up to 2 months.

mini meatballs
with minted yoghurt dip

MAKES 12 MEATBALLS (ABOUT 4 PORTIONS)

FOR THE MEATBALLS:
225 g/8 oz lean minced (ground)
   beef
40 g/1½ oz/¾ cup fresh white
   breadcrumbs
2.5 ml/½ tsp dried oregano or mixed
   herbs

1 egg yolk
Salt and freshly ground black pepper
15 ml/1 tbsp sunflower oil

FOR THE DIP:
45 ml/3 tbsp thick Greek-style
   yoghurt
2.5 ml/½ tsp bottled mint sauce

1 To make the meatballs, place the beef in a bowl with the breadcrumbs, herbs, egg yolk and a little salt and pepper. Work together with your hands until evenly mixed.

2 With dampened hands, shape the mixture into 12 small balls. Heat the oil in a large frying pan and cook the meatballs, turning them frequently, until they are well browned and cooked through. Drain on kitchen paper (paper towels) and leave to cool. Put a portion in a suitable container and chill in the fridge until ready to pack.

3 To make the dip, mix together the yoghurt and mint sauce. Pack in a tiny container and put in the lunchbox with the meatballs.

This delicious hot supper dish is equally good served cold the next day if you have a slice left over. Add favourite ingredients such as flaked tuna and diced tomato, or chopped chicken and sweetcorn instead of the ham and peas, if you prefer. For a vegetarian version, simply leave out the ham.

ham, potato and pea tortilla

MAKES 4–6 SERVINGS

30 ml/2 tbsp light olive oil
225 g/8 oz cold cooked new or other waxy potatoes, cut into small chunks
2.5 ml/½ tsp ground turmeric
1 small garlic clove, peeled and crushed

75 g/3 oz cooked ham, cut into small chunks
75 g/3 oz thawed frozen peas
4 eggs
15 ml/1 tbsp cream or milk
Salt and pepper

1   Heat the oil in a large non-stick frying, add the potatoes and sprinkle with the turmeric. Fry gently for 2 minutes, stirring all the time.

2   Add the garlic, ham and peas and mix well.

3   Whisk together the eggs, cream or milk and seasoning in a jug. Reduce the heat and slowly pour the mixture into the pan over the other ingredients. Cook over a very low heat for 10–15 minutes until golden underneath and almost set.

4   Loosen the edges of the tortilla with a palette knife, then carefully slide it out on to a large plate. Hold the frying pan over the top, then flip the tortilla back into the pan. Cook the other side for 5–6 minutes or until lightly browned.

5   Turn out the tortilla and cut it into wedges. Serve warm or cold.

6 Reserve a wedge for a packed lunch. Cool and chill it as quickly as possible, then wrap it in greaseproof (waxed) paper and foil or pack in sealed container.

Tip

It is important to keep food items such as cooked eggs really cool, so add an ice pack or a half-frozen drink to the lunchbox. Tortillas are not suitable for freezing.

The Cornish pasty was one of the first portable lunches, an all-in-one meal that was savoury at one end and sweet at the other. These have buttery pastry made with a combination of plain and self-raising flour, which gives it a lighter, softer texture, and a finely chopped vegetable and beef filling.

beef and vegetable pasties

MAKES 4

FOR THE PASTRY (PASTE):
75 g/3 oz/³/₄ cup plain (all-purpose) flour, plus extra for dusting
75 g/3 oz/³/₄ cup self-raising flour
A pinch of salt
75 g/3 oz/¹/₃ cup butter, cut into small pieces
30–45 ml/2–3 tbsp cold water
Beaten egg or milk to glaze

FOR THE FILLING:
1 small onion, finely chopped
¹/₂ medium potato, finely diced
1 small carrot, finely chopped
100 g/4 oz lean minced (ground) beef
15 ml/1 tbsp tomato ketchup (catsup)
30 ml/2 tbsp chopped fresh parsley
Salt and pepper

1 To make the pastry, sift the flours and salt into a bowl. Add the butter and rub into the flour with your fingertips until the mixture resembles fine breadcrumbs. Sprinkle the water evenly over the surface, then mix together to form a firm dough. Lightly knead for a few seconds on a floured surface, wrap in clingfilm (plastic wrap) and chill for 30 minutes.

2 Meanwhile, to make the filling, put all the ingredients in a bowl and mix together with your hands.

3 Divide the pastry into four equal portions. Roll out one to a 13 cm/5 in round, then cut out a neat circle, using a small plate or saucer as a guide. Spoon a quarter of the filling on to one half of the pastry, then dampen the edges with water.

4 Fold the pastry over to enclose the filling and press the edges together. Make small folds along the length to seal and crimp. Repeat to make three more pasties. Place on a baking (cookie) sheet, brush with beaten egg or milk, then make a small steam hole in each.

5 Bake the pasties in a preheated oven at 200°C/400°F/gas 6/fan oven 180°C for about 30 minutes or until the pastry is crisp and golden-brown. Leave on the baking sheet for a few minutes, then transfer them to a wire rack to cool.

6 When cold, wrap each pasty in clingfilm (plastic wrap) or foil and keep chilled until ready to pack. These will keep in the fridge for up to 2 days. Alternatively, freeze the wrapped pasties, preferably in a freezer container to prevent them being crushed. Defrost overnight in the fridge before packing. Use within 2 months.

Tip

If you're short of time, make the pasties with bought shortcrust pastry (basic pie crust).

Variations

Minced lamb and mint may be used instead of minced beef and parsley, if preferred. Try experimenting with other vegetables such as sweet potatoes or young turnips.

To make cheese and onion pasties, finely chop a small onion and fry in 15 g/½ oz/1 tbsp of butter for 5 minutes until softened. Mix with 100 g/4 oz of finely chopped potatoes and 75 g/3 oz/¾ cup of grated Cheddar cheese. Add some chopped fresh herbs, if liked.

These are similar to samosas but, as they are baked rather than deep-fried, their fat content is relatively low, which makes them a healthy as well as exciting addition in your child's lunchbox. Individually wrapped parcels can be frozen for up to 2 months, preferably in a container to prevent them being crushed.

mixed vegetable filo parcels

MAKES 6

15 ml/1 tbsp chutney (mango chutney is good)
1 small cooked potato, about 75 g/ 3 oz, finely diced
½ cooked carrot, diced

25 g/1 oz thawed frozen peas
A pinch of salt
1 sheet of filo pastry (paste), about 30 x 50 cm/12 x 20 in
15 ml/1 tbsp sunflower oil

1 To make the filling, chop up any large pieces of the chutney and place in a bowl with the vegetables. Season with a little salt (unless the vegetables have already been seasoned) and gently stir to mix everything together.

2 Place the sheet of filo on a board and cut it widthways into six strips, each about 30 cm/12 in long. Lightly brush with the oil. Take one of the strips and put a tablespoonful of the filling at one end. Fold the corner diagonally over the filling to make a triangle, then continue folding the strip over in triangles until you come to the end. 'Seal' the end with a little of the oil. Repeat with the remaining filo strips and filling.

3 Place the pastries on a non-stick baking (cookie) sheet and brush the tops with the remaining oil. Bake in a preheated oven at 200°C/400°F/gas 6/fan oven 180°C for 10–12 minutes, or until golden and crisp.

4 Transfer the pastries to a wire rack to cool. When they are cold, carefully wrap each in clingfilm (plastic wrap) or foil and keep chilled until ready to pack. These will keep in the fridge for up to 2 days, or may be frozen (see above).

Tip

These parcels are a good way to use up leftover cooked vegetables.

These little pies with a herb and tomato flavoured sausage filling are made with an egg-enriched pastry that can be rolled out thinly. Use a reduced-fat or premium sausagemeat for the best results. The pies can be wrapped individually and frozen, preferably in a container.

picnic pies with herb and tomato sausage filling

MAKES 6

FOR THE PASTRY (PASTE):
100 g/4 oz/1 cup plain (all-purpose) flour or a mixture of plain and wholemeal, plus extra for dusting
A pinch of salt
50 g/2 oz/¼ cup butter, chilled and diced
1 egg, lightly beaten
5 ml/1 tsp milk

FOR THE FILLING:
175 g/6 oz herby reduced-fat or premium pork sausagemeat
15 ml/1 tbsp chutney
15 ml/1 tbsp tomato ketchup (catsup)
Salt and pepper (optional)

1 To make the pastry, sift the flour and salt into a bowl. Add the butter and rub into the flour with your fingertips until the mixture resembles fine breadcrumbs. Reserve 10 ml/2 tsp of the beaten egg, then sprinkle the rest over the dry ingredients and mix to a dough. Lightly knead on a floured surface for a few seconds until smooth. Wrap in clingfilm (plastic wrap) and chill for 30 minutes.

2 Meanwhile, to make the filling, put the sausagemeat, chutney and ketchup in a bowl and season with a little salt and pepper, if liked. Using your hands, squeeze the mixture together until combined.

3 On a lightly floured surface, roll out just over half of the pastry until it is 3 mm/⅛ in thick. Using a 7.5 cm/3 in plain or fluted biscuit (cookie) cutter, stamp out six rounds of pastry. Gently press these into shallow patty tins, so that the pastry comes just above the tins to allow for shrinkage. Dampen the edges of the pastry by brushing lightly with cold water.

4 Put a rounded tablespoonful of the filling mixture into each pastry case, levelling it out with the back of the spoon. Roll out the remaining pastry and stamp out six rounds, using a 6 cm/2½ in plain or fluted cutter. Place on top of the filled pastry cases and press the edges together to seal.

5 Mix together the reserved beaten egg and the milk and brush over the tops of the pies to glaze. Make a steam hole in the top of each, then bake in a preheated oven at 190°C/375°F/gas 5/fan oven 170°C for 25–30 minutes until dark golden-brown. Leave in the tins for 10 minutes, then transfer to a wire rack to cool. When cold, wrap each in clingfilm (plastic wrap) or foil and keep chilled until ready to pack. These will keep in the fridge for up to 2 days, or may be frozen (see above).

Tips

For speed and convenience, you could use bought ready-rolled shortcrust pastry (basic pie crust).

If you can't get herby sausagemeat, buy plain and mix in 2.5 ml/½ tsp of dried mixed herbs.

A cross between a Cornish pasty and a pizza, these have a mildly spiced filling of minced turkey, vegetables and dried fruit. Minced chicken may be used if you prefer. The calzone can be wrapped individually and frozen, preferably in a container to prevent them being crushed, for up to 2 months.

spiced turkey and vegetable calzone

MAKES 6

15 ml/1 tbsp sunflower oil, plus extra for greasing
1 small onion, very finely chopped
1 garlic clove, peeled and crushed
225 g/8 oz minced (ground) turkey
A pinch of ground cinnamon
A pinch of ground turmeric
A pinch of ground cumin
75 ml/5 tbsp chicken or vegetable stock
1 medium carrot, coarsely grated
225 g/8 oz potato, peeled and cut into 1 cm/½ in dice

25 g/1 oz raisins or chopped dried apricots
15 ml/1 tbsp tomato purée (paste)
15 ml/1 tbsp chopped fresh parsley (optional)
Salt and pepper
250 g/9 oz packet of white bread or pizza dough mix
175 ml/6 fl oz/¾ cup warm water
Flour for dusting
Beaten egg to seal and glaze

1 Heat the oil in a frying pan, add the onion and garlic and cook over a medium heat for 3–4 minutes until beginning to soften. Add the turkey and cook for a further 3–4 minutes, stirring all the time.

2 Stir in the spices, then add the stock, carrot and potato. Reduce the heat, cover the pan with a lid and simmer for 10 minutes.

3 Stir in the dried fruit and tomato purée and cook, uncovered, for a few more minutes or until most of the stock has evaporated. Turn off the heat and stir in the parsley, if using. Season to taste with salt and pepper and leave to cool.

4 When the mixture is almost cool, empty the bread mix into a bowl and stir in the water to make a dough. Knead on a lightly floured surface for 2–3 minutes until smooth, or according to the packet instructions. Cover and leave to rest for 5 minutes, then divide into six equal pieces.

5 Roll out each piece to a 18 cm/7 in round. Divide the filling between the rounds, spooning it on to one side. Brush the edges with the beaten egg, then fold over to make a semi-circle. Press the edges together to seal, then crimp.

6 Transfer the calzone to a non-stick or lightly greased baking (cookie) sheet, cover with oiled clingfilm (plastic wrap) and leave in a warm place for 15 minutes until slightly risen. Uncover, glaze with the beaten egg and bake in a preheated oven at 200°C/400°F/gas 6/fan oven 180°C for 25 minutes until golden-brown.

7 Transfer to a wire rack to cool. When cold, wrap each in clingfilm (plastic wrap) or foil and chill until ready to pack. They will keep in the fridge for up to 2 days, or may be frozen (see above).

Brioche is delicious rich bread more usually associated with breakfast or teatime treats, but it can also be lovely with a savoury filling. It is extremely time-consuming to make but here packet bread mix is used, enriched with a little butter and milk. Individually wrapped brioches can be frozen for up to 2 months.

chicken and mushroom brioches

MAKES 6

FOR THE BRIOCHES:
15 g/½ oz/1 tbsp butter
120 ml/4 fl oz/½ cup milk
30 ml/2 tbsp cold water
250 g/9 oz packet of white bread or
   pizza dough mix
Flour for dusting

FOR THE FILLING:
15 g/½ oz/1 tbsp butter
10 ml/2 tsp sunflower oil, plus extra
   for greasing

1 shallot or ½ small onion, chopped
50 g/2 oz button mushrooms, wiped
   and sliced
1 cooked chicken breast, roughly
   chopped
5 ml/1 tsp Worcestershire sauce
1 small egg, lightly beaten
15 ml/1 tbsp chopped fresh parsley
Salt and pepper

1   To make the brioches, put the butter and half the milk in a small saucepan and heat gently until the butter has melted. Turn off the heat and add the remaining milk and the water. Empty the bread mix into a bowl and stir in the warm milk mixture to make a soft dough. Knead on a lightly floured surface for 2–3 minutes until smooth, or according to the packet instructions. Cover and leave to rise.

2   Meanwhile, to make the filling, heat the butter and oil in a small frying pan. Add the shallot and cook gently for 3–4 minutes until it is beginning to soften. Add the mushrooms and cook for 5 minutes until lightly browned and soft. Allow to cool for a few minutes, then tip into a food processor. Add the chicken and Worcestershire sauce and process for about 30 seconds until roughly chopped.

3 Reserve 15 ml/1 tbsp of the beaten egg. Add the rest to the food processor with the parsley and salt and pepper to taste. Scrape down the sides, then briefly process again until thoroughly mixed.

4 Knead the dough again for a few seconds to knock out any air, then divide into six equal pieces. Roll out each into a 13 cm/5 in round and put one-sixth of the filling in the middle. Pull up the sides of the dough around the filling and pinch together to seal.

5 Transfer the filled dough parcels to a lightly greased or non-stick baking (cookie) sheet, placing the joins underneath. Cluster them slightly apart, so that they will just touch as they rise – this helps to keep them soft. Cover with oiled clingfilm (plastic wrap) and leave for about 30 minutes until they are well risen and springy to the touch.

6 Remove the clingfilm and brush the tops with the reserved egg. Bake in a preheated oven at 200°C/400°F/gas 6/fan oven 180°C for 15–20 minutes or until golden-brown. Transfer to a wire rack and leave to cool. When cold, wrap each in clingfilm or foil and chill until ready to pack. These will keep in the fridge for up to 2 days, or may be frozen (see above).

Whether for slicing or spreading, spreads and pâtés are easy to eat and great for children who aren't so keen on the texture of meat or fish. Subtly flavoured with orange, this chicken pâté has a lovely creamy taste and texture and can be used thinly sliced in sandwiches.

creamy chicken and cream cheese pâté

MAKES ABOUT 350 G/12 OZ (4 SERVINGS)

275 g/10 oz boneless chicken breasts, skinned
100 g/4 oz packet of garlic and herb flavoured or plain soft or cream cheese

2 eggs
45 ml/3 tbsp double (heavy) cream
5 ml/1 tsp tomato purée
5 ml/1 tsp grated orange zest
Salt and freshly ground black pepper

1 Grease a 450 g/1 lb loaf tin and line it with greaseproof (waxed) paper or baking parchment.

2 Roughly chop the chicken and put it in a food processor with the cheese. Blend until fairly smooth. Add all the remaining ingredients and blend until smooth.

3 Spoon the mixture into the loaf tin, then give the tin a couple of sharp taps to remove any air pockets and to level the top. Cover with a piece of greased foil and transfer the tin to a small roasting dish. Pour in enough near-boiling water to come about half-way up the sides of the tin. Cooking in this way will stop the edges of the pâté becoming overcooked and dry.

4 Bake in a preheated oven at 160°C/325°F/gas 3/fan oven 145°C for 35 minutes or until firm to the touch. Allow the loaf to cool in the tin before turning it out. Wrap and store in the fridge for up to 2 days. Alternatively, it can be frozen in slices interleaved with non-stick baking parchment to keep them separate for up to 2 months.

Tip

Use an unwaxed orange or wash thoroughly before grating.

Many children refuse to eat fish, except in the form of the ubiquitous fish finger! This mild-tasting pâté will introduce them to the delicious flavour of smoked salmon and is great for spreading in sandwiches and rolls. Leave out the dill if you prefer. Smoked salmon trimmings are are ideal for this pâté.

smoked salmon and cream pâté

MAKES 4 SERVINGS

100 g/4 oz smoked salmon
10 ml/2 tsp lemon juice
50 g/2 oz/¹/₄ cup unsalted (sweet) butter, softened

30 ml/2 tbsp single (light) or double (heavy) cream
10 ml/2 tsp chopped fresh dill (dill weed)

1 Put the salmon in a food processor with the lemon juice and butter and blend until fairly smooth. Add the cream and dill, then process for a few more seconds.

2 Use the pâté straight away or spoon into a dish or dishes, cover and chill. Leave at room temperature for about 30 minutes before using to allow it to soften to a spreadable consistency.

Although perfect for vegetarians, this sliceable pâté is also good for meat-eaters and works well as one of the fillings in a double-decker sandwich, with sliced chicken in mayonnaise or crispy bacon as the other. It can be frozen in slices interleaved with non-stick baking parchment for up to 2 months.

lentil and
soft cheese pâté

MAKES ABOUT 225 G/8 OZ (4–6 SERVINGS)

Oil for greasing
225 g/8 oz/1¹/₃ cups red lentils
1 bay leaf
300 ml/¹/₂ pint/1¹/₄ cups hot
    vegetable stock
2.5 ml/¹/₂ tsp ground cumin

100 g/4 oz/¹/₂ cup soft cheese such
    as cream or curd (smooth
    cottage) cheese
4 ml/³/₄ tsp salt
4 eggs, lightly beaten

1 Grease a 450 g/1 lb loaf tin and line it with greaseproof (waxed) paper or non-stick baking parchment. Put the lentils in a sieve (strainer) and rinse well under cold running water. Tip into a saucepan and add the bay leaf and stock. If necessary, add a little boiling water so that the lentils are just covered.

2 Bring to the boil, reduce the heat and simmer for 40–45 minutes until the lentils are very soft and most of the liquid has been absorbed. Add the cumin about 5 minutes before the end of the cooking time. Turn off the heat and remove the bay leaf.

3 Add the cheese and salt and stir until the cheese has melted. Leave to cool for 5 minutes, then stir in the eggs. Spoon into the prepared tin, pressing the mixture into the corners. Level the top with the back of the spoon.

4 Cover with a piece of greased foil and transfer the tin to a small roasting dish. Pour in enough near-boiling water to come about half-way up the sides of the tin. Bake in a preheated oven at 180°C/350°F/gas 4/fan oven 160°C for 50 minutes or until firm to the touch. Allow the loaf to cool in the tin before turning it out. Wrap and store in the fridge for up to 4 days.

Nutritional note

Lentils are high in protein, starchy carbohydrate and fibre, but very low in fat. Make the most of their iron content by accompanying the pâté with a vitamin C-rich tomato salad or some fresh fruit.

A hot meal in a flask is a great winter warmer for older children – younger ones may find it difficult to pour. This big-filler soup is based on 'succotash' from the southern states of America, which traditionally includes butter beans. You could stir in a small drained can of these towards the end.

chicken and sweetcorn soup

MAKES 4 SERVINGS

1 uncooked or cooked skinless chicken breast
450 ml/³/₄ pint/2 cups hot chicken stock
25 g/1 oz/2 tbsp butter
1 onion, very finely chopped
2 back bacon rashers (slices), trimmed and diced

15 ml/1 tbsp plain (all-purpose) flour
200 g/7 oz/1 small can of sweetcorn, drained
30 ml/2 tbsp chopped fresh parsley
Salt and pepper
300 ml/¹/₂ pint/1¹/₄ cups milk

1 If using an uncooked chicken breast, add it to the stock in a saucepan, bring to the boil, then reduce the heat and simmer gently for 12–15 minutes until cooked through. Use a draining spoon to remove the chicken from the pan and set aside to cool.

2 Melt the butter in a saucepan, add the onion and cook gently for 8–10 minutes until softened. Stir in the bacon and cook for a further 2 minutes. Sprinkle the flour over and cook for 1 minute, stirring.

3 Gradually blend in the stock. Bring to the boil, stirring until thickened. Turn down the heat and simmer the soup for 5 minutes. Cut the chicken into bite-sized pieces and add to the soup with the sweetcorn, parsley and salt and pepper to taste.

4 Stir in the milk and heat the soup gently until it is piping hot, but do not boil. Rinse out the flask with hot water (this helps to keep the soup warm until lunchtime), pour in a portion, seal and pack.

Tips

If you're planning to freeze the soup in portions, divide it into small individual containers after step 3. Defrost a portion in the fridge overnight, then simmer for 1 minute before adding 75 ml/3 fl oz of milk. Heat until piping hot and pour into a warmed flask.

A squat, wide-necked flask is ideal, but check that it retains heat well as some 'children's' flasks aren't very effective.

Puréeing vegetables often seems to make them more attractive to children. Send this soup to school with a small pot of grated cheese or some crunchy croûtons to sprinkle over when serving. This is a healthy low-fat soup, so make sure that you include other more substantial foods in the lunchbox.

creamy
vegetable soup

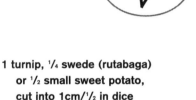

MAKES 4 SERVINGS

15 g/¹/₂ oz/1 tbsp butter, preferably
  unsalted (sweet)
1 onion, finely chopped
600 ml/1 pint/2¹/₂ cups vegetable
  stock
1 potato, cut into 1 cm/¹/₂ in dice
1 carrot, cut into 1 cm/¹/₂ in dice

1 turnip, ¹/₄ swede (rutabaga)
  or ¹/₂ small sweet potato,
  cut into 1cm/¹/₂ in dice
15 ml/1 tbsp tomato purée
30 ml/2 tbsp chopped fresh parsley
Salt and pepper

1 Melt the butter in a saucepan, add the onion and cook gently for 7–8 minutes until softened but not browned. Pour in the stock and bring to the boil. Add the remaining vegetables to the pan as they are prepared.

2 Cover and simmer gently for 25–30 minutes or until tender. Turn off the heat, stir in the tomato purée, then leave to cool for a few minutes.

3 To make a completely smooth soup, ladle it into a liquidiser and blend until very smooth. Alternatively, for a chunkier texture, purée half the soup, then stir into the remaining unpuréed soup.

4 Return the soup to the pan, stir in the parsley and season with salt and pepper. Reheat a portion until bubbling. Rinse out the flask with hot water (this helps to keep the soup warm until lunchtime), pour in the soup, seal and pack. The remaining portions can be frozen in individual small containers. Defrost in the fridge overnight, then reheat until piping hot before pouring into the warmed flask.

Tips

For non-vegetarians, you could make the soup more substantial by adding leftovers such as finely diced chicken or ham after puréeing.

If the soup is a little thick, or a creamier texture is preferred, stir in a little milk when reheating.

A squat, wide-necked flask is ideal, but check that it retains heat well as some 'children's' flasks aren't very effective.

Shop-bought peanut butter is an easy option but it often contains unwanted hydrogenated oil, high amounts of sugar and preservatives. Making your own is quick, simple and fun for the kids to watch. Because it contains no preservatives, this peanut butter should be eaten within 2 weeks of making.

home-made
peanut butter

MAKES ABOUT 150 ML/¹/₄ PINT/²/₃ CUP

175 g/6 oz/1¹/₂ cups unsalted
roasted shelled peanuts

30 ml/2 tbsp groundnut (peanut) or
sunflower oil
1.5–2.5 ml/¹/₄–¹/₂ tsp salt

1 Put the peanuts in a food processor and process for a few seconds until roughly chopped. Drizzle the oil over the top and sprinkle with the smaller amount of salt. Briefly process again until the mixture is a coarse paste.

2 Taste and season with a little more salt, if liked, then process for a few seconds more for crunchy peanut butter, or a further 1–2 minutes for smooth. Spoon into a small clean jam jar or bowl and store in the fridge.

Tip

To roast shelled unsalted peanuts, place them on a baking (cookie) sheet and cook in a preheated oven at 200°C/400°F/gas 6/fan oven 180°C for 8–10 minutes. Allow to cool slightly, then rub off the skins before using.

SWEET TREATS
AND CAKES

While it's a good idea to reduce the number of high-sugar foods your child eats, moderation and variety are key words for healthy eating. Cakes, biscuits and other bakes needn't contain a massive amount of sugar or fat and can make a positive contribution to your child's diet. When you bake at home, you know what's going in and you can add lots of beneficial ingredients such as whole grains, fruits and nuts to boost the nutritional value of these treats.

Food intolerances need not deprive your child of a baked treat. Chewy Oat and Syrup Flapjacks are suitable for those on a wheat-free diet, and Carob Chip and Honey Cookies for those who need a gluten-free or lactose-free one.

These moist, yoghurt-enriched sponge slices are dotted with chopped apricots, a great source of iron and dietary fibre. With their crunchy oat-and-seed topping, they make a satisfying and energy-sustaining bake. They may be individually wrapped and frozen, or will keep in an airtight container for up to 3 days.

apricot crumble slices

MAKES 12 SLICES

FOR THE TOPPING:
75 g/3 oz/³/₄ cup plain (all-purpose) flour
25 g/1 oz/¹/₄ cup porridge oats
25 g/1 oz/¹/₄ cup sunflower seeds
50 g/2 oz/¹/₄ cup light soft brown sugar
50 g/2 oz/¹/₂ cup butter or sunflower margarine, melted, plus extra for greasing

FOR THE SPONGE:
200 g/7 oz/1³/₄ cups self-raising flour
5 ml/1 tsp ground cinnamon
2.5 ml/¹/₂ tsp baking powder
A pinch of salt
100 g/4 oz/¹/₂ cup caster (superfine) sugar
100 g/4 oz/²/₃ cup chopped ready-to-eat dried apricots
40 g/1¹/₂ oz/3 tbsp butter or sunflower margarine, melted
200 ml/7 fl oz/scant 1 cup Greek-style yoghurt
15 ml/1 tbsp milk
2 eggs, lightly beaten
340 g/12 oz jar of apricot jam

1 To make the topping, put the dry ingredients in a bowl, pour the melted butter or margarine over and stir together with a fork to make a crumbly mixture. Grease and line the base of a 28 × 18 cm/ 11 × 7 in traybake tin with baking parchment.

2 To make the sponge, sift the flour, cinnamon, baking powder and salt into a bowl. Stir in the sugar and apricots, then make a well in the middle. Mix together the butter or margarine, yoghurt, milk and eggs. Add to the well in the dry ingredients, then fold together until combined. Spoon into the prepared tin and level out.

3 Beat the jam in a bowl until softened. Drop small spoonfuls of jam over the top of the sponge, then spread out into an even layer. Sprinkle the topping mixture over the jam. Bake in a preheated oven at 180°C/350°F/gas 4/fan oven 160°C for about 40 minutes until golden brown. Leave to cool in the tin, then cut into 12 slices.

Because metal and wooden skewers aren't ideal in the school canteen (even the most sensible child can be accidentally jostled), a drinking straw is used instead. Buy thin, non-bendy ones for the best results. Make sure that the length of the straw isn't greater than the lunchbox.

mixed fresh fruit kebabs

MAKES 1 OR 2

¹/₂ crisp eating (dessert) apple	50 g/2 oz large seedless red or
¹/₂ ripe, but not too soft, pear	white grapes
	30 ml/2 tbsp orange juice

1 Core, but do not peel, the apple and pear and cut the flesh into bite-size cubes. Make a hole through each piece of fruit using a thick skewer, then toss in the orange juice to coat.

2 Thread the fruit on to a straw through the holes. Wrap the kebabs in clingfilm (plastic wrap) and keep chilled until ready to pack.

Tip and variations

If necessary, cut the straws in half and make two shorter kebabs so they fit into the lunchbox easily.

Make tropical kebabs with fruits such as mango and fresh or canned pineapple chunks. Bananas also taste good, but will discolour slightly.

Most children love jelly and combining it with fruit turns it into a nutritious dessert. Choose your child's favourite fruit and jelly combination; try fresh raspberries and halved seedless grapes with raspberry jelly or chopped tinned fruit in natural juices with peach or lemon jelly.

fresh and fruity
orange jelly

MAKES 1 PORTION

¼ packet of orange jelly (jello)
About 50 ml/2 fl oz boiling water

1 small or medium orange
About 50 ml/2 fl oz orange juice

1 Cut the jelly into small pieces and place in a heatproof measuring jug. Pour over enough boiling water to come up to the 75 ml/3 fl oz mark, then stir until the jelly has dissolved. Leave until just cool.

2 Working on a plate to catch the juices, cut the peel and white pith from the orange using a sharp knife, then cut out the segments. Place them in a small plastic container.

3 Stir any juices on the plate into the jelly, then add enough orange juice to reach the 150 ml/¼ pint/⅔ cup mark. Stir well and pour over the orange segments. Cover and leave in the fridge to set.

Tips

Recipes containing jelly are not suitable for freezing or for vegetarians.

Avoid using fresh pineapple as it contains an enzyme that prevents jelly setting.

Evaporated milk contains the concentrated goodness of fresh milk and gives this simple strawberry mousse a lovely frothy texture and creamy flavour. Make sure that the evaporated milk is really well chilled, so that it whisks to maximum volume. Recipes containing jelly are not suitable for freezing.

fluffy strawberry mousse

MAKES 2 PORTIONS

½ packet of strawberry jelly (jello)
About 150 ml/¼ pint/²/₃ cup boiling water

120 ml/4 fl oz/½ cup chilled evaporated milk
A few fresh strawberries, quartered (optional)

1 Cut the jelly into small pieces and place in a heatproof measuring jug. Pour over enough boiling water to come up to the 150 ml/ ¼ pint/²/₃ cup mark, then stir until the jelly has dissolved. Leave until just cool.

2 Pour the evaporated milk into a bowl and whisk until it is really light and fluffy. Slowly pour in the jelly, still whisking. Stir in the strawberries, if using.

3 Divide the mousse between two suitable containers. Cover and leave in the fridge to set. Keep chilled until ready to pack.

Tip

Recipes containing jelly are not suitable for vegetarians.

Try to include some fruit in your child's lunchbox every day. An apple, orange or banana is an easy addition but sometimes you could be a bit more adventurous and pack this attractive dessert. When making fruit salads, try to use fully ripe fruit so that it is deliciously sweet; you can then reduce the sugar.

fresh green fruit salad

MAKES 1 PORTION

15 ml/1 tbsp lime cordial
30 ml/2 tbsp cold water
5 ml/1 tsp caster (superfine) sugar
50 g/2 oz seedless white grapes, halved

1 kiwi fruit, peeled, halved lengthways and sliced
1 small slice of ogen melon, peeled, seeded and cut into small chunks

1 Put the lime cordial, water and sugar in a jug and stir briskly until the sugar has dissolved.

2 Put the fruit in a suitable container and pour the lime syrup over. Cover and keep chilled until ready to pack.

Tip

This salad is not suitable for freezing but will keep chilled for 2 days in the fridge.

Make this when these luscious fruits are in season and plentiful. Fruits such as plums and cherries are wonderful when raw, but can be messy to eat and easily stain clothes. Here, they are prepared and very lightly cooked. This recipe can be kept in the fridge for 2 days but is not suitable for freezing.

plum and cherry compôte

MAKES 2 PORTIONS

15 ml/1 tbsp smooth 'no bits' plum jam (conserve)
10 ml/2 tsp caster (superfine) sugar
15 ml/1 tbsp apple juice

2 ripe red plums, halved and stoned (pitted)
100 g/4 oz fresh cherries, stoned

1 Put the jam, sugar and apple juice in a saucepan and heat gently, stirring occasionally, until the jam has melted and the sugar dissolved.

2 Chop the plums into bite-sized pieces and cut each cherry in half. Add to the pan and bring the mixture to the boil. Gently simmer for 1 minute, then turn off the heat.

3 Leave to cool, then pack in two small lidded containers and keep chilled until ready to pack. Use within 2 days of making.

These light-textured, mildly spiced little cakes are very moist and don't taste of carrots. You can leave them without icing, or add a tiny dollop of cream cheese frosting, as here. Use chopped walnuts or pecans instead of the raisins, if you prefer. You can easily halve this recipe to make a batch of six.

moist carrot
cup cakes

MAKES 12

FOR THE CAKES:
50 g/2 oz/¹/₃ cup raisins
100 g/4 oz/¹/₂ cup caster (superfine)
    sugar
90 ml/6 tbsp sunflower oil
2 eggs, lightly beaten
1 large carrot, peeled and grated
100 g/4 oz/1 cup self-raising flour
2.5 ml/¹/₂ tsp baking powder
5 ml/1 tsp ground cinnamon

5 ml/1 tsp ground ginger

FOR THE FROSTING:
100 g/4 oz/¹/₂ cup full-fat soft cream
    cheese
5 ml/1 tsp clear honey
5 ml/1 tsp lemon juice or a few
    drops of vanilla essence (extract)
10 ml/2 tsp icing (confectioners')
    sugar (optional)

1 To make the cakes, scatter the raisins in the bases of 12 paper cake cases (cupcake papers) in a bun tin (patty pan). Put the sugar and oil in a bowl and beat them together with a wooden spoon for a few seconds. Gradually add the eggs, beating well after each addition.

2 Stir in the carrot, then sift the flour, baking powder and spices over the mixture. Gently fold in with a large metal spoon. Divide the mixture equally between the cake cases.

3 Bake in a preheated oven at 190°C/375°F/gas 5/fan oven 170°C for 15 minutes or until well risen, golden-brown and firm to the touch. Leave in the tin for 5 minutes, then transfer to a wire rack to cool.

4 To make the frosting, beat together the cream cheese, honey and lemon juice or vanilla essence. Cut a slice from the top of each cake and spoon a little of the frosting into the centre. Replace the slice of cake on top. Sift a little of the icing sugar over the cakes, if liked.

5 Carefully wrap each cake in clingfilm (plastic wrap) or foil and chill until ready to pack. These will keep in the fridge for up to 2 days, or may be frozen for up to 2 months. They defrost quickly so can be packed from frozen in the morning and will be ready to eat by lunchtime.

Nutritional note

Carrots are rich in beta-carotene, which helps to protect cells against damage by free radicals. Older, darker carrots have more beta-carotene than young carrots.

This is a simple all-in-one mixture that can be divided and given several different flavourings for variety. The cakes will keep for 5 days, or may be individually frozen for up to 2 months. They defrost quickly so can be packed from frozen and will be ready to eat by lunchtime.

mixed mini cakes
with fruit, fudge and chocolate

MAKES 12

100 g/4 oz/¹/₂ cup soft tub margarine
100 g/4 oz/¹/₂ cup caster (superfine) sugar
2 eggs
100 g/4 oz/1 cup self-raising flour

40 g/1¹/₂ oz chopped dried fruit such as sultanas (golden raisins), chopped apricots, glacé (candied) cherries
25 g/1 oz/¹/₄ cup chocolate drops
25 g/1 oz/¹/₄ cup chopped fudge

1 Place 12 paper cake cases (cupcake papers) in a bun tin (patty pan). Put the margarine, sugar, eggs and flour in a large bowl and beat well for 2–3 minutes until the mixture is well blended and smooth.

2 Use a quarter of the mixture to half-fill three of the cake cases. Spoon another quarter into a second bowl and gently fold in the fruit. Use this to half-fill three more cake cases. Divide the remaining mixture between the two bowls. Stir the chocolate drops into one and the fudge pieces into the other. Use these to half-fill the rest of the cake cases.

3 Bake the cakes in a preheated oven at 200°C/400°F/gas 6/fan oven 180°C for 15 minutes or until well risen, golden-brown and firm to the touch. Leave to cool in the tin for a few minutes, then transfer to a wire rack to cool.

4 Carefully wrap each cake in clingfilm (plastic wrap) or foil and chill until ready to pack, or freeze (see above).

Wholemeal bakes can be a bit heavy-going for children. These moist muffins are made with part wholemeal, part white flour for a wholesome yet light texture. The muffins can be wrapped individually and frozen, preferably in a container so they don't get crushed, and will keep for up to 1 month.

banana and orange muffins

MAKES 6

75 g/3 oz/³/₄ cup self-raising flour
50 g/2 oz/¹/₂ cup self-raising wholemeal flour
5 ml/1 tsp baking powder
A pinch of salt
40 g/1¹/₂ oz/3 tbsp caster (superfine) sugar

2 ripe bananas, about 225 g/8 oz peeled weight
Finely grated zest of 1 orange
1 egg, lightly beaten
50 ml/2 fl oz sunflower oil
50 ml/2 fl oz milk
10 ml/2 tsp demerara sugar

1 Grease a 6-cup muffin tin or line with paper muffin cases. Mix together the flours, baking powder, salt and sugar in a large bowl, then make a well in the middle. Roughly mash the bananas, then combine with the orange zest, egg, oil and milk.

2 Pour into the dry ingredients and stir together quickly until just combined. Two-thirds fill each muffin case with the mixture, then sprinkle the tops with the demerara sugar.

3 Bake in a preheated oven at 200°C/400°F/gas 6/fan oven 180°C for 20–25 minutes or until well risen and golden. Leave in the tin for 5 minutes, then transfer to a wire rack to cool.

4 Carefully wrap each muffin in clingfilm (plastic wrap) or foil and keep chilled until ready to pack. These will keep in the fridge for 1 day. If you decide to freeze them (see above), they defrost quickly so can be packed frozen in the morning and will be ready to eat by lunchtime.

Nutritional note

Bananas have a high potassium content, vital for the functioning of nerves and muscles in the body.

These are made by the traditional quick and simple muffin method, but the result is more like a light, soft-textured sponge. The muffins only keep in the fridge for a day, but they can be wrapped individually and frozen, preferably in a container so they don't get crushed, and will keep for up to 1 month.

raspberry yoghurt muffins

MAKES 12

250 g/9 oz/2¼ cups self-raising flour
5 ml/1 tsp bicarbonate of soda (baking soda)
100 g/4 oz/½ cup caster (superfine) sugar

2 eggs, lightly beaten
75 ml/5 tbsp sunflower oil
150 g/5 oz carton of raspberry-flavoured yoghurt
15 ml/1 tbsp lemon juice
150 g/5 oz fresh raspberries

1   Grease a 12-cup muffin tin or line with paper muffin cases. Mix together the flour, bicarbonate of soda and sugar in a large bowl, then make a well in the middle.

2   Mix together the eggs, oil, yoghurt and lemon juice in a jug. Pour into the hollow in the dry ingredients, add the raspberries, then stir together just until combined. Quickly divide the mixture between the cases, filling them almost to the top.

3   Bake in a preheated oven at 190°C/375°F/gas 5/fan oven 170°C for 15–20 minutes or until well risen and golden. Leave in the tin for 5 minutes, then transfer to a wire rack to cool.

4   Carefully wrap each muffin in clingfilm (plastic wrap) or foil and keep chilled until ready to pack. If you freeze them (see above), they can be packed frozen in the morning and will be ready to eat by lunchtime.

These bite-sized moist muffins are studded with chocolate chips. They are the perfect size for adding to lunchboxes as a special treat. The same mixture can also be used to make six large muffins instead of 18 mini ones. Bake them at the same temperature but increase the cooking time to 18–20 minutes.

mini chocolate-chip muffins

MAKES 18 MINI MUFFINS

125 g/4½ oz/generous 1 cup self-raising flour
2.5 ml/½ tsp baking powder
25 g/1 oz/1 tbsp butter, cut into small cubes
40 g/1½ oz/3 tbsp light soft brown sugar

50 g/2 oz/½ cup milk chocolate chips
1 egg
100 ml/3½ fl oz/scant ½ cup milk
5 ml/1 tsp vanilla essence (extract)

1 Grease 18 holes in mini-muffin tins or line with mini-muffin cases. Mix together the flour and baking powder in a large bowl, then rub in the butter until the mixture resembles fine breadcrumbs.

2 Stir in the sugar and chocolate chips. Lightly beat the egg in a jug, then stir in the milk and vanilla essence. Pour into the dry ingredients and stir together until just combined. Quickly divide the mixture between the cases, filling them almost to the top.

3 Bake in a preheated oven at 200°C/400°F/gas 6/fan oven 180°C for 8–10 minutes or until well risen and golden. Leave in the tins for 5 minutes, then transfer to a wire rack to cool.

4 Carefully wrap each muffin in clingfilm (plastic wrap) or foil and keep chilled until ready to pack. They will keep in the fridge for 1 day. Alternatively, freeze the individually wrapped muffins, preferably in a container to protect them, for up to 1 month. They can be packed frozen and will be ready to eat by lunchtime.

These are packed with dried fruit, nuts, oats and seeds and make perfect lunchbox fodder to give your child an energy boost and keep her alert for the rest of the day. They are also a healthy alternative to reaching for the biscuit tin. They contain no wheat so are suitable for those on a wheat-free diet.

fruit and nut
energy bars

MAKES 12

175 g/6 oz/1 cup no-need-to-soak dried apricots, chopped
75 g/3 oz/³/₄ cup almonds, chopped
50 g/2 oz/¹/₂ cup ground almonds
300 g/11 oz/2³/₄ cups porridge oats
50 g/2 oz/¹/₃ cup raisins
100 g/4 oz/1 cup sunflower or pumpkin seeds or a mixture of both

50 g/2 oz/¹/₂ cup sesame seeds
50 g/2 oz/¹/₂ cup milk (sweet) or plain (semi-sweet) chocolate chips
225 g/8 oz/1 cup demerara sugar
175 g/6 oz/³/₄ cup butter
150 g/5 oz/scant ¹/₂ cup clear honey

1 Grease and line the base of a 23 cm/9 in square baking tin with non-stick baking parchment. Put the apricots, chopped almonds, ground almonds, oats, raisins, seeds and chocolate chips in a large bowl and stir together to mix.

2 Gently heat the sugar, butter and honey in a saucepan, stirring frequently until the butter has melted and the sugar has dissolved. Bring to a gentle simmer and cook for 3 minutes.

3 Turn off the heat and, when the bubbles subside, pour the melted mixture over the dry ingredients and stir until thoroughly mixed. Transfer the mixture to the prepared tin and press down firmly with the back of the spoon.

4 Bake in a preheated oven at 190°C/375°F/gas 5/fan oven 170°C for 20 minutes until golden-brown. Put the tin on a wire rack to cool. When cold, chill in the fridge for 1 hour.

5 Turn out on to a chopping board and peel off the lining paper. Cut the square in half, then cut each half into six slices. Wrap them separately in clingfilm (plastic wrap) or foil and store in an airtight container until ready to pack.

Tip

These will keep for up to 5 days, or may be frozen, preferably in a freezer container to protect them, for up to 2 months. They can be packed from frozen and will be ready to eat by lunchtime.

Although these sticky flapjacks are relatively high in fat and sugar, only a small piece should be enough to satisfy even the sweetest tooth. Vary these by adding some chopped ready-to-eat dried apricots, prunes or dates, plus a few seeds such as sunflower, pumpkin, sesame and linseeds.

chewy oat and syrup flapjacks

MAKES 15

175 g/6 oz/³/₄ cup butter
175 g/6 oz/³/₄ cup demerara sugar

30 ml/2 tbsp golden syrup
225 g/8 oz/2 cups porridge oats

1 Lightly grease a 28 × 18 cm/11 × 7 in traybake tin and line with greaseproof (waxed) paper or non-stick baking parchment. Put the butter, sugar and syrup in a large saucepan and gently heat until melted, stirring occasionally.

2 Turn off the heat, then add the oats to the pan and stir to combine. Spoon the mixture into the prepared tin and level the top with the back of the spoon.

3 Bake in a preheated oven at 160°C/325°F/gas 3/fan oven 145°C for 25 minutes or until golden-brown. Remove from the oven and leave for 10 minutes. Cut the mixture into 15 pieces, then leave to cool completely in the tin.

4 Store the flapjacks in an airtight container for up to 4 days. Wrap each in clingfilm (plastic wrap) or foil before packing or freezing, preferably in a freezer container to protect them, for up to 1 month. They can be packed from frozen and will be ready to eat by lunchtime.

Nutritional note

Oats are an excellent source of soluble fibre, which helps to slow the absorption of carbohydrate into the bloodstream, resulting in a more gentle rise and fall in blood sugar levels.

Here a layer of chopped bananas and dates is sandwiched between a chewy coconut and muesli mixture. It's a recipe that an older child may want to help you make, and it's good to encourage an interest in healthy cooking. They are not suitable for freezing but will keep in an airtight container for up to 3 days.

date and banana muesli squares

MAKES 15

175 g/6 oz/1¹/₂ cups unsweetened 'luxury' muesli
175 g/6 oz/1¹/₂ cups porridge oats
100 g/4 oz/1 cup desiccated (shredded) coconut
100 g/4 oz/1 cup butter

100 g/4 oz/¹/₂ cup light muscovado sugar
175 g/6 oz/¹/₂ cup clear honey or maple syrup
2 small ripe bananas
Juice of ¹/₂ lemon
100 g/4 oz/²/₃ cup stoned (pitted) dates, chopped

1 Grease and line the base of a 28 × 18 cm/11 × 7 in traybake tin with baking parchment. Put the muesli, porridge oats and coconut in a bowl and mix together.

2 Gently heat the butter, sugar and honey in a small saucepan until the butter has melted and the sugar dissolved. Pour over the dry ingredients and mix together until combined. Press half the mixture over the base of the prepared tin.

3 Thinly slice the bananas and mix with the lemon juice. Add the dates and mix again. Scatter the banana and date mixture over the muesli layer in the tin. Top with the remaining muesli mixture, pressing down firmly.

4 Bake in a preheated oven at 180°C/350°F/gas 4/fan oven 160°C for about 25 minutes until golden-brown. Leave to cool in the tin, then turn out on to a board and cut into 15 squares.

5 Wrap each in clingfilm (plastic wrap) or baking parchment, then foil before packing.

A traybake tin is a worthwhile investment and can be used for all sorts of cakes and bakes. It's an ideal size for cutting into large or small squares and slices. For a banana and walnut traybake, substitute 2 ripe mashed bananas for the apples and 100 g/ 4 oz/1 cup chopped walnuts for the apricots.

fresh apple and apricot traybake

MAKES 10–14 SLICES

100 g/4 oz/¹/₂ cup butter, softened
150 g/5 oz/scant ³/₄ cup light
　muscovado sugar
2 eggs, lightly beaten
225 g/8 oz/2 cups self-raising flour
2.5 ml/¹/₂ tsp ground cinnamon
2 eating (dessert) apples, peeled,
　cored and coarsely grated

100 g/4 oz/²/₃ cup ready-to-eat dried
　apricots, chopped
30 ml/2 tbsp milk

FOR THE ICING:
50 g/2 oz/¹/₃ cup icing
　(confectioners') sugar
15 ml/1 tbsp lemon juice

1 Grease and line the base of a 28 × 18 cm/11 × 7 in traybake tin with baking parchment. Put the butter and sugar in a large bowl and beat together until light and fluffy. Add the eggs, a little at a time, beating well after each addition.

2 Sift the flour and cinnamon over the mixture, then add the apples, apricots and milk. Gently fold in until thoroughly mixed. Spoon into the prepared tin and level the top with the back of the spoon.

3 Bake in a preheated oven at 180°C/350°F/gas 4/fan oven 160°C for 45 minutes or until a skewer inserted into the middle comes out clean.

4 Leave the cake in the tin for 10 minutes, then turn out on to a wire rack and leave to cool. Peel off the lining paper when cold.

5 To make the icing, sift the icing sugar into a bowl and stir in the lemon juice. Drizzle over the top of the cake in zig-zags and leave to set.

6 Cut the cake into slices. Wrap each in clingfilm (plastic wrap) or baking parchment, then foil before packing. Alternatively, freeze the individually wrapped slices, preferably in a freezer container to protect them, for up to 1 month. They can be packed from frozen and will be ready to eat by lunchtime.

Nutritional note

Dried apricots are a useful source of both iron and calcium. Use them in recipes or pack a few as an extra snack to help boost intake of these essential minerals.

Home-made gingerbread improves with keeping and this one will keep well for up to 10 days, becoming stickier with time. Individually wrapped slices can also be frozen. You can make a lighter gingerbread by increasing the proportion of syrup to molasses.

hand-made
sticky gingerbread

MAKES 12 SLICES

100 g/4 oz/¹/₂ cup butter or
margarine, softened
100 g/4 oz/¹/₂ cup light muscovado
sugar
2 eggs
175 g/6 oz/¹/₂ cup golden (light
corn) syrup
100 g/4 oz/¹/₃ cup molasses or
black treacle

225 g/8 oz/2 cups plain
(all-purpose) flour
5 ml/1 tsp ground mixed spice
5 ml/1 tsp ground cinnamon
2.5 ml/¹/₂ tsp bicarbonate of soda
(baking soda)
30 ml/2 tbsp milk

1 Grease and line the base of a deep 18 cm/7 in square baking tin with baking parchment.

2 Put the butter or margarine, sugar, eggs, syrup and molasses or treacle in a bowl and beat together with a wooden spoon until blended.

3 Sift the flour and spices over the mixture and fold in. Blend together the bicarbonate of soda and milk, then stir in. Pour into the prepared tin.

4 Bake in a preheated oven at 160°C/325°F/gas 3/fan oven 145°C for 1 hour, then turn down the oven to 150°C/300°F/gas 2/fan oven 135°C and cook for a further 10–20 minutes or until firm to the touch. Leave in the tin for 10 minutes, then turn out on to a wire rack to cool.

5 When cold, cut into 12 slices. Wrap each in clingfilm (plastic wrap) or foil and store in an airtight container until ready to pack.

Nutritional note

Molasses is a by-product of sugar refining and varies in richness and colour. The very dark blackstrap molasses contains the most nutrients and is rich in iron, calcium and zinc.

These oat and raisin cookies are really versatile; follow the basic recipe, then add the flavourings of your choice. I have included some ideas below but you may well think of others. They also make a wonderful addition to a party tea and there should be something there to please every child!

smart oat and raisin cookies

MAKES 15

75 g/3 oz/¹/₃ cup butter, softened
100 g/4 oz/¹/₂ cup light muscovado sugar
1 egg, lightly beaten

100 g/4 oz/1 cup self-raising flour
50 g/2 oz/¹/₂ cup oatmeal
100 g/4 oz/²/₃ cup raisins

1 Put the butter and sugar in a large bowl and beat together until light and fluffy. Gradually add the egg, beating well after each addition. Sift the flour over, add the oatmeal and raisins and gently fold and stir into the mixture.

2 Drop heaped teaspoonfuls of the mixture on to three lightly greased or lined baking (cookie) sheets, leaving space between the mixture for the cookies to spread.

3 Bake in a preheated oven at 180°C/350°F/gas 4/fan oven 160°C for 12–15 minutes or until golden-brown. Allow to cool for a few minutes on the sheets, then transfer to a wire rack to cool completely.

4 Wrap each cookie in clingfilm (plastic wrap) or foil before packing. They will keep in an airtight container for up to 4 days. Alternatively, these may be frozen, preferably in a container to protect them, for up to 2 months. They can be packed from frozen and will be ready to eat by lunchtime.

Nutritional note

Raisins are a useful source of iron. Include some vitamin-C rich fruit or juice in the lunchbox to help the body absorb this.

Variations

Add extra flavour by beating in the finely grated zest of 1 small orange with the butter and sugar, or by sifting in 5 ml/1 tsp of ground mixed spice or ginger with the flour.

To make chocolate and raisin oat cookies, substitute 15 ml/1 tbsp of cocoa (unsweetened chocolate powder) for the same quantity of flour and a 25 g/ 1 oz tube of Smarties or white, milk (sweet) or plain (semi-sweet) chocolate chips for 25 g/1 oz of the raisins.

To make cherry and apricot oat cookies, omit the raisins and add 75 g/ 3 oz/^{1}/$_2$ cup of chopped dried apricots and 25 g/1 oz of chopped glacé (candied) cherries.

An ideal way to give your child a small chocolate treat, these cookies are half-dipped in chocolate, so there is an uncoated end to hold on to for easy eating. The individually wrapped cookies can be frozen for up to 1 month, preferably in a container to prevent them from being crushed.

chocolate-dipped cocoa cookies

MAKES 10

50 g/2 oz/¹/₂ cup plain (all-purpose) flour
15 ml/1 tbsp cocoa (unsweetened chocolate) powder
25 g/1 oz/2 tbsp caster (superfine) sugar
1.5 ml/¹/₂ tsp baking powder

25 g/1 oz/2 tbsp unsalted (sweet) butter, softened
10 ml/2 tsp golden (light corn) syrup
50 g/2 oz/¹/₂ cup milk chocolate chips
15 ml/1 tbsp sugar sprinkles

1 Line a baking (cookie) sheet with baking parchment. Sift the flour, cocoa, sugar and baking powder into a mixing bowl. Add the butter and syrup, then stir the ingredients together.

2 Work the mixture with your hands until it combines to form a dough. Wrap and chill in clingfilm (plastic wrap) for 20 minutes.

3 Roll out the dough to a rectangle about 20 × 10 cm/8 × 4 in. Trim the edges, then cut into 10 × 2 cm/4 × ³/₄ in fingers.

4 Transfer the cookies to the baking sheet and bake in a preheated oven at 180°C/350°F/gas 4/fan oven 160°C for 12–15 minutes. Leave them to cool on the baking sheet for 5 minutes, then transfer to a wire rack to cool completely.

5 Put the chocolate chips in a small heatproof bowl and set over a pan of hot water until melted (alternatively, melt briefly in the microwave). Half-dip the cookies, one at a time, then place on baking parchment. Immediately after dipping, scatter each with a few sugar sprinkles. Leave to set.

6 Store the cookies in a cool place in an airtight container for up to 4 days. Wrap each in clingfilm (plastic wrap) or baking parchment, then foil before packing. Alternatively, these may be frozen (see above).

Tip

These can be packed frozen in the morning and will be ready to eat by lunchtime.

Food intolerances need not deprive your child of home-made cakes and cookies. These can be enjoyed by anyone on a gluten-free or lactose-free diet. The individually wrapped cookies can be frozen for up to 1 month, preferably in a container to prevent them from being crushed.

carob chip and honey cookies

MAKES 10

175 g/6 oz/1½ cups gluten-free flour, plus extra for dusting
75 g/3 oz/⅓ cup vegetable margarine

25 g/1 oz/2 tbsp light muscovado sugar
75 g/3 oz/½ cup carob chips
20 ml/4 tsp clear honey
10 ml/2 tsp demerara sugar

1 Put the flour in a mixing bowl and rub in the margarine until the mixture resembles fine breadcrumbs. Stir in the muscovado sugar and carob chips.

2 Drizzle the honey over, then stir until the mixture comes together into a dough. Roll out on a lightly floured surface to about 8 mm/ ⅓ in thick.

3 Stamp out rounds using a plain or fluted 6 cm/2½ in biscuit (cookie) cutter. Transfer to a non-stick baking (cookie) sheet or a sheet lined with baking parchment. Prick the cookies all over with a fork and sprinkle with the demerara sugar.

4 Bake in a preheated oven at 180°C/350°F/gas 4/fan oven 160°C for 12–15 minutes or until firm. Leave to cool on the baking sheet for 5 minutes, then transfer to a wire rack to cool completely.

5 Store the cookies in a cool place in an airtight container for up to 4 days. Wrap each in clingfilm (plastic wrap) or baking parchment, then foil before packing. Alternatively, these may be frozen (see above).

Tip

These can be packed frozen in the morning and will be ready to eat by lunchtime.

These delicious cookies, laden with coconut, fruit and chocolate, are crunchy on the outside but have a soft, chewy centre. They don't cook so much as dry out, so they can be made last thing at night, then left in the oven overnight. By the morning they will be ready for wrapping and packing.

overnight fruit cookies

MAKES 10

1 egg white
100 g/4 oz/¹/₂ cup caster (superfine) sugar
50 g/2 oz/¹/₂ cup desiccated (shredded) coconut
50 g/2 oz/¹/₂ cup ground almonds

75 g/3 oz/¹/₂ cup chopped dried fruit such as apricots, tropical fruit or glacé (candied) cherries
75 g/3 oz/³/₄ cup milk (sweet) or plain (semi-sweet) chocolate chips

1 Line a baking (cookie) sheet with non-stick baking parchment. Put the egg white in a large bowl and whisk until stiff peaks form. Add the sugar a spoonful at a time, whisking well between each addition. Gently fold in all the remaining ingredients.

2 Place 10 spoonfuls of the mixture on to the baking sheet, spacing them slightly apart.

3 Put the cookies in a preheated oven at 220°C/425°F/gas 7/fan oven 200°C. Turn off the oven and leave the cookies overnight (or for at least 7 hours during the day) without opening the door.

4 Store the cookies in a cool place in an airtight container for up to 4 days. Wrap each in clingfilm (plastic wrap) or baking parchment, then foil before packing. Alternatively, the wrapped cookies may be frozen, preferably in a container to protect them, for up to 1 month. They defrost quickly so can be packed from frozen in the morning.

SAVOURY TREATS AND BREADS

For those who don't have a sweet tooth, I have included some savoury treats, including Cheese-crusted Mini Scones and Sausage and Tomato Sauce Spirals – useful additions to the lunchbox for those with extra-large appetites. Finally, when you've run out of bread, or feel like making your own, there's a selection of quick and simple breads to choose from.

These little cheesy scones make great little savoury additions to any packed lunch. As soon as they are cool, split them in half and spread them with butter, even if you intend to freeze them, then wrap them individually. This will save time during the early-morning rush to leave the house on time.

cheese-crusted mini scones

MAKES ABOUT 15

175 g/6 oz/1½ cups self-raising flour, plus extra for dusting
2.5 ml/½ tsp baking powder
A pinch of salt
25 g/1 oz/2 tbsp butter, cut into small pieces, plus extra for spreading

50 g/2 oz/½ cup finely grated Cheddar cheese
100 ml/3½ fl oz/scant ½ cup milk
Beaten egg or milk for glazing

1 Sift the flour, baking powder and salt into a mixing bowl. Add the butter and stir to coat, then rub in with the fingertips until the mixture resembles fine breadcrumbs. Stir in two-thirds of the cheese.

2 Add the milk and mix with a blunt knife to make a soft dough. Lightly knead on a floured surface for a few seconds until smooth, then roll out to about 1 cm/½ in thick.

3 Using a 4 cm/1½ in round or fun-shaped biscuit (cookie) cutter, stamp out small shapes and place them on a lightly greased baking (cookie) sheet. Re-roll the trimmings and stamp out more shapes. Brush all the shapes with beaten egg or milk, then sprinkle with the reserved cheese.

4 Bake the scones in a preheated oven at 220°C/425°F/gas 7/fan oven 200°C for 7–8 minutes until well risen and golden-brown. Transfer them to a wire rack to cool.

5 When cool, wrap each scone in clingfilm (plastic wrap) or foil and store in an airtight container for up to 2 days, until ready to pack. Alternatively, the individually wrapped scones may be frozen, preferably in a container to protect them, for up to 2 months. They can be packed from frozen in the morning and will be ready to eat by lunchtime.

Muffins don't have to be sweet; these delicious cheesy ones are lovely and light and incredibly quick and easy to make.

Although it may seem unusual to add sugar to a savoury muffin, it brings out the cheese flavour and improves the texture. This is another recipe that would also be great for a party.

savoury light cheese muffins

MAKES 9 STANDARD OR 25 MINI MUFFINS

250 g/9 oz/2¼ cups plain (all-purpose) flour
15 ml/1 tbsp baking powder
A pinch of salt
30 ml/2 tbsp caster (superfine) sugar

75 g/3 oz/¾ cup grated hard cheese such as Cheddar
1 egg
250 ml/8 fl oz/1 cup milk
75 ml/5 tbsp sunflower oil

1 Grease the muffin tins or line with paper muffin cases. Sift the flour, baking powder, salt and sugar into a mixing bowl, then stir in the cheese. Make a hollow in the middle of the dry ingredients.

2 Using a fork, beat together the egg, milk and oil in a jug. Pour into the hollow, then stir just until combined, taking care not to over-mix. Divide the mixture between the muffin cases.

3 Bake in a preheated oven at 200°C/400°F/gas 6/gan oven 180°C for 20 minutes for the larger muffins and 12–15 minutes for the smaller ones, until well risen and lightly browned. Leave in the tins for a few minutes, then transfer to a wire rack to cool.

4 Wrap each muffin in clingfilm (plastic wrap) or foil and chill until ready to pack. These will keep in an airtight container for up to 2 days. Alternatively, the individually wrapped muffins may be frozen, preferably in a container to protect them, for up to 6 weeks. They can be packed from frozen in the morning and will be ready to eat by lunchtime.

Variation

For pizza-style muffins, stir in 25 g/1 oz of chopped peperoni sausage, 25 g/1 oz of chopped sun-dried tomatoes and 2.5 ml/$^{1}/_{2}$ tsp of dried mixed herbs with the cheese.

These are a quick and simple alternative to sausage rolls. A sheet of ready-rolled puff pastry may be used if preferred. Your child may want to help you make these. They make good party food – but you should make double the quantity as they will be popular with adults as well as children!

sausage and tomato sauce spirals

MAKES ABOUT 20

225 g/8 oz puff pastry (paste)
100 g/4 oz reduced-fat or premium
  sausagemeat

15 ml/1 tbsp tomato ketchup
  (catsup)
A pinch of dried mixed herbs
Salt and pepper

1 Roll out the pastry to a rectangle, approximately 20 × 25 cm/8 × 10 in, then trim the edges. Put the sausagemeat, ketchup and herbs in a bowl and season with salt and pepper. Mix together with your hands. Spread this mixture as thinly and evenly as possible to within 1 cm/½ in of the pastry edges.

2 Lightly brush one of the long edges of the pastry with a little water, then roll from the other side, like a Swiss roll, to enclose the filling. Cut into 1 cm/½ in thick slices and arrange on a baking (cookie) tray, spacing them slightly apart.

3 Bake in a preheated oven at 220°C/425°F/gas 7/fan oven 200°C for 12–15 minutes, until puffy and dark golden-brown. Leave on the baking tray for 5 minutes, then transfer to a wire rack to cool.

4 Wrap each sausage spiral in clingfilm (plastic wrap) or foil and store in an airtight container in the fridge until ready to pack. These will keep for up to 3 days, or may be frozen, preferably in a container to protect them, for up to 2 months and then packed from frozen in the morning. They will be ready to eat by lunchtime.

These delicious wheat and oat biscuits are perfect for packed lunches. They're also good with creamy cheeses after a meal. Using a combination of wholemeal flour and oatmeal provides a healthy dose of dietary fibre, particularly useful if your child is usually a fan of white bread sandwiches and rolls.

savoury wheat and oat shortbread

MAKES ABOUT 15

175 g/6 oz/1½ cups stoneground wholemeal flour, plus extra for dusting
50 g/2 oz/½ cup medium oatmeal
5 ml/1 tsp baking powder

A pinch of salt
100 g/4 oz/½ cup butter, cut into small pieces
30 ml/2 tbsp caster (superfine) sugar

1 Put the flour, oatmeal, baking powder and salt in a mixing bowl and stir together. Add the butter and rub in until the mixture resembles fine breadcrumbs. Stir in the sugar.

2 Using your hands, gently work the mixture to a firm dough. (Alternatively, put all the ingredients in a food processor and process until it just comes together.)

3 Roll out the dough on a lightly floured surface to about 5 mm/¼ in thick. Stamp out rounds with a plain or fluted 7.5 cm/3 in biscuit (cookie) cutter. Place on an ungreased baking (cookie) sheet, spacing the biscuits slightly apart.

4 Bake in a preheated oven at 190°C/375°F/gas 5/fan oven 170°C for 10–12 minutes until darkening at the edges. Leave on the baking sheet for a couple of minutes, then transfer to a wire rack to cool.

5 When cold, wrap each biscuit in clingfilm (plastic wrap) or foil and store in an airtight container until ready to pack. They will keep for up to 5 days. Alternatively, the individually wrapped biscuits may be frozen, preferably in a container to protect them, for up to 2 months and packed from frozen in the morning. They will be ready to eat by lunchtime.

When you have the time and inclination, or the bread bin is empty, you can follow this quick and easy recipe and bake a batch of rolls. These soft baps are lovely and light, with an almost unnoticeable amount of wholemeal flour. For smaller appetites, make 12 baps instead of 8.

soft white milk baps

MAKES 8

350 g/12 oz/3 cups strong white bread flour
100 g/4 oz/1 cup strong or plain (all-purpose) wholemeal or brown flour
5 ml/1 tsp salt

15 ml/1 tbsp caster (superfine) sugar
5 ml/1 tsp easy-blend dried yeast
300 ml/½ pint/1¼ cups tepid semi-skimmed milk
20 ml/4 tsp sunflower or olive oil, plus extra for greasing

1 Sift the flours, salt and sugar into a large bowl, tipping in any bran left in the sieve (strainer). Stir in the yeast, then make a well in the middle and pour in the milk and oil. Stir with a wooden spoon, gradually mixing in the flour to make a soft dough.

2 Turn out on a lightly floured surface and knead the dough for 10 minutes until smooth and elastic. Place the dough in a large, lightly greased or floured bowl and cover with clingfilm (plastic wrap). Leave to rise in a warm place for about 1 hour or until doubled in size.

3 Turn out the risen dough on to a floured work surface and knock it back with your knuckles. Divide into eight equal pieces and shape each into a round. Place on a greased baking (cookie) sheet, spacing them slightly apart, then press down on each to make a flattened round. Cover with a piece of oiled clingfilm and leave to rise in a warm place for 30–40 minutes or until doubled in size again (don't worry if the baps are touching each other; this will keep them soft when they are baked).

4 Remove the clingfilm and brush the tops of the rolls with milk or sprinkle them with a little white or wholemeal flour. Bake in a preheated oven at 220°C/425°F/gas 7/fan oven 200°C for 10–12 minutes or until well risen and golden-brown. Transfer to a wire rack to cool.

5 When cold, store the baps in an airtight container for up to 3 days. Alternatively, wrap the baps individually in clingfilm or pack them in a freezer container or freezer bag and use within 3 months – you can split and butter them first for easy use. Fill and pack the rolls from frozen.

Tip

If you have a breadmaker, use it to mix and knead the dough.

Variation

You can vary the recipe by changing the proportions of flour or by adding cheese, herbs, nuts or seeds. Wholemeal flour absorbs more liquid than white, so if using more than in this recipe you will need to add an extra tablespoonful or two of milk.

A cross between a roll and a scone, these can be filled with sliced meat or cheese or spreads such as hummus. However, because they already contain cheese and egg, they are nutritious served simply split and buttered as a lunchbox treat. They also make a great after-school snack.

cheese and oatmeal rolls

MAKES 8

225 g/8 oz/2 cups self-raising flour, plus extra for dusting
10 ml/2 tsp baking powder
A pinch of salt
75 g/3 oz/³/₄ cup medium oatmeal

50 g/2 oz/¹/₂ cup mature Cheddar cheese, finely grated
1 egg
75 ml/5 tbsp milk
60 ml/4 tbsp sunflower or light olive oil, plus extra for greasing

1 Sift the flour, baking powder and salt into a mixing bowl. Stir in the oatmeal and cheese and make a well in the middle.

2 Beat together the egg and milk in a jug. Reserve 15 ml/1 tbsp of the mixture and set aside. Stir the oil into the remaining egg and milk and add it to the dry ingredients. Mix to a soft dough.

3 Cut the dough into eight pieces. Lightly knead each piece on a floured surface for just a few seconds until smooth, then shape into a flattened ball.

4 Place on a lightly greased baking (cookie) sheet and brush the tops with the reserved egg and milk mixture. Bake in a preheated oven at 200°C/400°F/gas 6/fan oven 180°C for 15 minutes or until well risen and golden-brown. Transfer to a wire rack to cool.

5 When cold, store in an airtight container for up to 3 days. The rolls can also be individually wrapped in clingfilm (plastic wrap) and frozen in a container for up to 3 months. Fill and pack the rolls from frozen.

Cornmeal is made by grinding dried maize into tiny pieces and you may also find it on supermarket shelves labelled 'instant polenta'. Cut the round into slices and butter them thinly before packing and if you find you have any left over it can be served with salads to make a lunch or light supper.

quick and easy cornbread

MAKES ONE 20 CM/8 IN SQUARE LOAF

175 g/6 oz/1½ cups cornmeal (maize meal)
150 g/5 oz/1¼ cups self-raising flour
5 ml/1 tsp baking powder
45 ml/3 tbsp caster (superfine) sugar

2.5 ml/½ tsp salt
150 ml/¼ pint/⅔ cup plain yoghurt
120 ml/4 fl oz/½ cup semi-skimmed milk
60 ml/4 tbsp sunflower or light olive oil, plus extra for greasing
1 egg, lightly beaten

1   Grease and line the base of a 20 cm/8 in square baking tin with baking parchment. Put the cornmeal, flour, baking powder, sugar and salt in a large bowl and stir to mix. Make a well in the middle.

2   Mix together the yoghurt, milk, oil and egg. Pour into the dry ingredients and mix to a soft dough. Shape into a rough round and press into the tin.

3   Bake in a preheated oven at 200°C/400°F/gas 6/fan oven 180°C for 25–30 minutes until firm and golden-brown. Leave in the tin for 10 minutes before turning out on to a wire rack to cool. Store in an airtight container or wrapped in foil and eat within 3 days.

Note

This recipe is not suitable for freezing.

This quick bread, based on traditional Irish soda bread, is made without yeast. Buttermilk provides good amounts of vitamin B$_2$ and calcium, but if you don't have any you can use semi-skimmed milk mixed with 15 ml/1 tbsp lemon juice instead. This recipe is not suitable for freezing.

simple
soda bread

MAKES 6 WEDGES

300 g/11 oz/2^3/$_4$ cups plain (all-purpose) white flour, plus extra for dusting
225 g/8 oz/2 cups plain (all-purpose) wholemeal or brown flour

5 ml/1 tsp bicarbonate of soda (baking soda)
2.5 ml/^{1}/$_2$ tsp salt
300 ml/^{1}/$_2$ pint/1^1/$_4$ cups buttermilk
Oil for greasing

1 Sift the flours, bicarbonate of soda and salt into a large mixing bowl, adding the bran left in the sieve (strainer). Make a well in the middle.

2 Pour in the buttermilk, then stir with a wooden spoon to make a soft dough. Bring the dough together with your hands and knead on a lightly floured surface for a few seconds until smooth.

3 Shape the dough into a rounded dome about 20 cm/8 in in diameter. Place on a greased baking (cookie) sheet and mark into six wedges, cutting about half-way down into the dough. Bake in a preheated oven at 200°C/400°F/gas 6/fan oven 180°C for 30 minutes or until well risen and browned. The loaf should sound hollow when tapped on the base. Transfer to a wire rack and leave to cool.

4 When cold, cut into wedges and use within 1 day of making.

INDEX

Vegetarian recipes are marked (V)
Recipes containing nuts (N)

adolescents 7
allergies 15–16
amino acids 9
antioxidants 12, 61, 67
apples
  fresh apple and apricot
    traybake 116–17
apricots 117
apricot crumble slices 100
  fresh apple and apricot
    traybake 116–17
attentiveness 7, 10

bacon
  classic club sandwich 37
  crispy bacon brioche fingers 51
  egg and bacon pitta pocket with
    cress 44
balanced diet 9–14, 19
bananas 109
  banana and orange muffins 109
  banana smoothie 23
  date and banana muesli squares 115
baps
  big brunch bap with sausage 48
  soft white milk baps 134–35
beans
  butter bean, cottage cheese and
    watercress dip (V) 67
  easy bean burritos with corn
    tortillas (V) 41
beansprouts 72
  crunchy oriental salad (V) 65
  sprouting beans for salads and
    sandwiches (V) 72
beef
  beef and vegetable pasties 80–1
  mini meatballs with minted yoghurt
    dip 77
biscuits *see* cookies
blood sugar levels 7, 10, 22, 114
bread 24, 32
  cheese and oatmeal rolls 136

quick and easy cornbread 137
simple soda bread 138
soft white milk baps 134–35
see also individual types
breakfast 22–3
brioche
  chicken and mushroom brioches 88–9
  crispy bacon brioche fingers 51
bulghar wheat 59
  tabbouleh with feta cheese (V) 58–9
butter bean, cottage cheese and
  watercress dip (V) 67

cakes
  apricot crumble slices 100
  banana and orange muffins 109
  chewy oat and syrup flapjacks 114
  date and banana muesli squares 115
  fresh apple and apricot
    traybake 116–17
  hand-made sticky
    gingerbread 118–19
  mini chocolate-chip muffins 111
  mixed mini cakes with fruit, fudge
    and chocolate 108
  moist carrot cup cakes 106–7
  raspberry yoghurt muffins 110
  see also cookies
calcium 14
calzone
  spiced turkey and vegetable
    calzone 86–7
carbohydrates 10
  importance at breakfast 23
carob chip and honey cookies 124–25
carrots 61, 107
  Dutch cheese and carrot
    salad (V) 62
  moist carrot cup cakes 106–7
  vegetable crisps (V) 71
cheese (cheddar)
  cheese and oatmeal rolls 136
  cheese and onion pasties (V) 81
  cheese-crusted mini scones 128–29
  savoury light cheese
    muffins 130–31